FOOD
family
STYLE

FOOD
family
STYLE

SIMPLE AND TASTY RECIPES
FOR EVERYDAY LIFE

Leigh Oliver Vickery

Revell
a division of Baker Publishing Group
Grand Rapids, Michigan

Published by Revell
a division of Baker Publishing Group
P.O. Box 6287, Grand Rapids, MI 49516-6287
www.revellbooks.com

Printed in the United States of America

Library of Congress Cataloging-in-Publication Data
Vickery, Leigh Oliver.
    Food family style : simple and tasty recipes for everyday life / Leigh Oliver
Vickery.
        p.   cm.
    Includes index.
    ISBN 978-0-8007-2114-5 (pbk.)
    1. Cooking, American. 2. Families. I. Title.
TX715.V53 2012
641.5973—dc23   2012010119

The internet addresses, email addresses, and phone numbers in this book are accurate
at the time of publication. They are provided as a resource. Baker Publishing Group
does not endorse them or vouch for their content or permanence.

Published in association with the literary agency of Alive Communications, Inc.,
7680 Goddard Street, Suite 200, Colorado Springs, Colorado 80920, www.alive
communications.com.

The recipe for the Chipotle Chicken Tostadas pictured on the front cover is found
on p. 135.

12 13 14 15 16 17 18   7 6 5 4 3 2 1

Dedicated to my mother and best friend B. J. Smith,
who has helped me discover the great loves of my life:

Jesus Christ,
my family,
a good book,
a busy kitchen, and
dark chocolate.

Because of you, dear Mama, I believe.

Contents

Introduction
One Big Happy Table

I would like to pretend that mealtime at our house is always peaceful.

In my imaginary world that exists somewhere between Mary of the House of Jesus and Martha of the House of Stewart, I picture my husband and two teenage sons smiling and smelling fresh, seated at our kitchen table while I serve them a hot meal.

And although I don't actually wear any of these in real life, my dream outfit is a freshly pressed pleated skirt, pastel twinset, and a strand of antique pearls.

After appropriate oohing and aahing over the meal I created, we hold hands and take turns thanking God for his blessings. Equally as important, everybody chews with their mouths closed.

Alas, the reality is much closer to these recent real-life examples around our house:

I had forgotten to go to the grocery store the day before, and we were out of everything we usually eat for breakfast.

I said, "We don't have any eggs. Or bacon. Or bread. Or milk. We're having beef tacos for breakfast. You liked them just fine last night. And you better be thankful. Remember there are kids all over the world who will not eat today."

My son hollered, "Then send them the leftover tacos! I just want some American chocolate milk!"

And another night, I was greeted with this as I put dinner on the table:

"MOM, why did you make this again? You know I hate chicken chop suey! If you make me eat this, I will commit chicken chop suicide!"

(And no, this cookbook does not include the recipe for the dreaded chicken chop suicide.)

This next one might be the best. As I was finishing preparing a talk for MOPS International's convention in Nashville last year, my husband called upstairs to the office-slash-playroom, "Leigh, supper is on the table. We're waiting for you to come join us."

This was my response, bellowed down the stairwell:

"I don't have time to eat tonight! Don't you remember I fly out tomorrow to give my talk on the importance of family mealtime?!"

Needless to say, as soon as the words left my mouth, I was busted. And the hoots and snickers from around the table downstairs told me how ridiculous I must have sounded.

Kids love it when Mom has to apologize, don't they?

But for all those crazy moments at mealtime, there are many wonderful ones we have enjoyed around our kitchen table. I don't think life feels any better than when we are eating together—laughing, talking, and letting our conversations wander where they will.

And although it doesn't seem logical that simply sharing food with one another would be as important (if not more so) as teaching your kids practical reasons to stay off drugs and to study hard in school, the evidence is clear. Children of families who regularly eat together are more likely to grow up into mature, responsible, and happy people.

But you don't have to take my word for it; there are countless studies coming out of Harvard, Columbia, and other prestigious research facilities that say eating together several times a week is one of the absolute best ways to help children stay on the right path, help marriages remain intimate, and even mend broken relationships.

The more often families eat together, the less likely kids are to smoke, drink, do drugs, get depressed, develop eating disorders, and consider suicide. The flip side is also true. The more often you sit down, eat with your family, and just talk, the more likely your children are to do well in school, delay having sex, eat their vegetables, learn big words, and know which fork to use.

In our home, we try to sit down together to eat at least four nights a week. Yes, it takes work to get everyone's schedule to somehow align and to get food on the table. And yes, many nights it doesn't work out as well as I imagined.

But we try, and I have seen that the more often we make time to eat together, the better our family relationships become. We have learned how to work together (when the boys are hungry enough, they don't mind helping!), we have learned better table manners, and we have learned so much about our boys' thoughts and ideas we might never have known.

And the laughter that comes from full stomachs and the sense of security a family can give—I wouldn't trade that for anything! Even without all the statistics and studies showing that the family dinner is a crucial part of our society, you know in your heart that when good food and laughter are around your table, it simply feels great. It feels right.

I could elaborate on why I think sharing food with people we love is so powerful, but Robert Farrar Capon, an American Episcopal priest and author, says it much better than I can:

> For all its greatness, the created order cries out for further greatness still. The most splendid dinner, the most exquisite food, the most gratifying company, arouse more appetites than they satisfy. They do not slake man's thirst for being; they whet it beyond all bounds.[1]

I have come to understand that time around the dinner table with people I love is sacred, and the table is our prelude to much better things to come.

One day, my hope is that you and I will be together, laughing and enjoying God's wonderful creation as we were meant to—around one big happy table.

I wanted to write *Food Family Style* to help you enjoy your time in the kitchen and your family's time around the table. Getting food on the table and everyone seated at the same time will always take work, but before you know it, your family will look forward to these moments—and the magic of meatloaf and mashed potatoes.

1. Robert Farrar Capon, *The Supper of the Lamb* (New York: Smithmark, 1996), 188–90.

Let's Begin

I was in my car when I first received a phone call from Jean Blackmer at MOPS International. (My car really is my second home and office, complete with snacks, toilet paper, and internet service.) It was a dream come true to be asked to help create this cookbook for MOPS (Mothers of Preschoolers). Well, to be honest, I had not even known to dream for an opportunity this extraordinary. I am grateful to my loving Father who knows how to care for me and bless me in ways I don't even know how to imagine.

MOPS is an amazing organization, as many of you have experienced. There's nothing better than having a community of other mothers to lean on and learn from when the days feel long and tempers feel short. And although my boys are older now, one of my very best friends came from the time in our lives when we both had young children and just needed to check in with each other (several times a day) to make sure we were not going crazy or making huge parenting mistakes.

MOPS gives you a wonderful place to create friendships with women who are doing their best—just like you—to be great moms, wives, and friends.

And as basic as it sounds, part of our biggest responsibilities in taking care of our families is simply feeding them! It doesn't seem like that big of a deal, but you might be startled to realize your child will eat an average of 19,710 times by the time he or she turns eighteen. Yikes! That's a lot of meals to get on the table . . . which is where this cookbook comes into the picture.

I hope this cookbook will help inspire you to make mealtime a priority in your home. I worked with other MOPS moms across the country to find tried-and-true recipes kids and families love, and I have also included many of my friends' and family's favorites to help make your time in the kitchen fun, easy, and delicious!

Throughout each section, you will find helpful, easy-to-read icons to help you plan and prepare meals. Look for these symbols at the end of each recipe to help you choose what's best for your family.

2X = Doubles Easily

These recipes can be easily doubled to feed a crowd—or a few hungry teenagers.

❄ = Freezes Well

These recipes freeze well, making it easier to plan ahead.

Ⓖ = Gluten Free

These recipes do not have wheat as an ingredient. Some foods have hidden sources of gluten or were processed in a plant where wheat is used, so please always read the labels on the ingredients you choose.

♥ = Healthful

These recipes are more health-conscious choices, cutting fat or calories, and were created with attention to healthier ingredient options.

★ = MOPS Favorite

These recipes are MOPS favorites—and some are from MOPS moms.

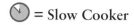 = Slow Cooker

These recipes are suitable for preparing in a slow cooker, and slow cooker instructions are included in the recipe directions.

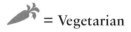 = Vegetarian

These recipes are vegetarian.

Food Family Style also has tips for stocking a perfect pantry, getting your kids involved in the kitchen, and talking around the table, as well as a few complete menu ideas for special occasions. Each recipe should feed a family of four, unless it says otherwise.

My hope is that *Food Family Style* will become your go-to cookbook for family mealtimes. Yes, cooking does take planning and a bit of effort, but in a short time, I am confident you will feel God's blessings upon your family as you enjoy the pleasure of good food and family conversations.

There are few things in life as sacred as sitting together around the table and inviting our Creator to join us as we give thanks for what he has given us. May you feel his love and his pleasure as you go about your kitchen, changing what seems ordinary into something extraordinary for your family: a place full of love called home.

Hope to see you around the table!

Leigh

CHAPTER 1

Kids in the Kitchen

*Cooking is like love. It should be entered into
with abandon or not at all.*

Julia Child

My favorite people in the world to cook with are children. I love their imaginations, creativity, willingness to take a risk, and ability to laugh when things don't turn out exactly as planned!

The kitchen is a wonderful playground for you and your child to create, experiment, and play, while also offering the benefit of immediate results. I love seeing confidence and joy light up a child's face when a bowl of flour, sugar, eggs, butter, and chocolate magically becomes a pan of warm brownies. Sure, you're going to make a lot of messes, but what is life if not a little messy? In the end, you realize life tastes pretty good. And the beauty of being made in the image of our Father, the ultimate Creator, is that the more we create, the more like our true selves we become.

You may not have thought about cooking with your kids as a place to teach more than the basic skills of how to get food on the table, but it's really a beautiful setting for many lessons:

Learning to be patient
Maintaining a sense of humor
Handling failure

Working as a team

Following through on a task

Mastering health and cleanliness skills

Reading and following instructions

Developing math, science, and vocabulary skills

Enjoying a sense of accomplishment

Using your imagination

Developing healthy eating habits

And like any playground, it's best to have a few rules and boundaries in place to keep everyone safe and playing happily.

The first and most important rule of learning to cook is to HAVE FUN! Having fun should be the foundation of every kitchen activity you begin with your children. If it's not fun or if they fear failure, then they'll never discover the joy and pleasure of cooking and eating what they've created. It will seem like just another chore, and they might miss out on one of God's greatest blessings.

Two of the many things I appreciate about my mother are that she gave me a lot of freedom in the kitchen and never, ever told me I was making too big of a mess or that what I created was a disaster. Believe me, I was (and am) messy and made many disasters (think baked iceberg salad!), but she continually encouraged me and built my confidence. This is a wonderful gift you can give your own children, and here's an important secret I've learned: if I let my kids help plan and cook the menu, they are much more likely to eat what they've prepared. This even works with green beans!

Here are a few practical suggestions for you to go over with your child to keep your time in the kitchen running smoothly:

1. Ask permission!

Make sure your child knows to always ask your permission before beginning any project in the kitchen. Hey, why not suggest to them that you want to be their helper in the kitchen? You will learn things together, and the best part is this: at the end, you will have something yummy to enjoy together as a family.

2. Be safe!

Before getting started, make sure you both read our "Safety Tips for Kids" for the kitchen (see p. 20).

3. Be prepared!

You and your child need to read through the recipe you want to make. Take this time to look up any words or techniques you don't know. You might even learn about another country's culture as you experiment with ethnic recipes. It's also very important to gather together everything you need—both ingredients and tools—before you start cooking. You don't want to be halfway through the recipe and realize you're missing something!

4. Be clean!

Cleaning is a big part of cooking, although it's not nearly as fun. Not only is it safer to keep a tidy kitchen, but if you clean as you go along, then when you're ready to sit down and enjoy what you've cooked you won't have mountains of dishes to worry about.

5. Have fun!

Back to our first rule. Most of all, remember to enjoy your time in the kitchen and learn to do things the way you enjoy! Experiment and make changes that work for your tastes, and be sure to write those changes next to the recipe so you'll remember next time.

Safety Tips for Kids

Properly Handwash

Always wash your hands before cooking or making a snack. Use warm water and plenty of soap. Wash the tops and bottoms of your hands, between your fingers, and under your fingernails. Scrub for at least twenty seconds. Rinse your hands with warm water, and dry them with a clean towel. You also need to repeat this handwashing immediately after handling any raw meat of any kind.

Prevent Germs

Wash vegetables and fruits in clean water (no soap) before you eat them. Wash your hands immediately after you touch raw poultry, meat, fish, or eggs, which can contain bacteria that can make you ill. Keep work areas and countertops clean by washing them with warm water and soap. Raw meat should be cut and prepared on a separate surface from fruits and vegetables, and that surface should be immediately washed with hot water and soap. Store leftover food in the refrigerator; don't leave it on the counter.

Use Caution around the Stove and Oven

Never use a stove or oven unless an adult has given you permission and instructed you how to use it. Be sure to keep towels, paper towels, and pot holders away from the burners. Don't wear loose clothing or long sleeves while cooking, as clothing can catch fire if it touches a hot burner. Turn pan handles toward the rear of the stove so the pan won't be accidentally knocked over by somebody walking by. Turn the stove or oven off when you're done cooking, and remember that the burner will stay hot for several minutes after it has been turned off.

Practice Microwave Safety

Although microwave ovens can be safer and easier to use than the stove, there are still certain dangers. Ask your parents what containers are safe to use in the microwave. Avoid plastic bags and plastic tubs because the plastic can melt. Don't use brown paper bags or Styrofoam takeout containers. And NEVER use aluminum foil or metal in the microwave. Remember that food is very hot when it's removed from the microwave, even if it doesn't look hot. Stir food before you eat it, as some parts might be hotter than others.

The Lord is good to me
For this I thank the Lord
For giving me the things I need
The sun, the rain, and the appleseed
The Lord is good to me.

—The Johnny Appleseed Song

Island Smoothies

2 cups	pineapple juice
1 cup	ice cubes
⅓ cup	nonfat milk
¼ cup	honey

Combine all ingredients in a blender. Make sure the blender lid is on tight before you turn it on. Process on high speed until smooth and frothy, about 45 seconds. Pour into 4 glasses and serve.

Hit the Trail Mix

2 cups	raisins
2 cups	candy-coated chocolate pieces such as plain M&Ms
2 cups	pretzel sticks or small pretzel twists
2 cups	sunflower nuts
2 cups	toasted oat "o" cereal such as Cheerios

Combine all ingredients in a large mixing bowl, stir, and divide mixture evenly between 16 resealable sandwich bags (about ¾ cup each). Store bags in freezer. Just pull out, wait 10 minutes, and you'll be ready to hit the trail!

Gluten Free Snack Mix

3 cups	gluten free rice cereal squares
3 cups	popped popcorn
½ cup	mixed nuts
3 Tbs.	vegetable oil
⅓ cup	Parmesan cheese, grated
2 tsp.	garlic salt
2 tsp.	chili powder

Preheat oven to 350°F. Combine cereal, popcorn, and nuts in large bowl. Drizzle with oil and stir to coat. Sprinkle with Parmesan cheese, garlic salt, and chili powder, stirring to coat evenly. Spread mixture on large, ungreased baking sheet. Bake 15 minutes, turning once. Cool and store in an airtight container. Serves about 6.

Cheesy Barbecue Popcorn

2 Tbs.	unsalted butter, melted
½ tsp.	chili powder
½ tsp.	garlic salt
¼ tsp.	onion powder
8 cups	popped popcorn
¼ cup	grated Parmesan cheese

Combine first four ingredients. Pour over popcorn, stirring to coat well. Sprinkle with cheese and stir again. Makes 8 servings.

MOPS Favorite: Peanut Butter Pretzels

1 (10 oz.) bag	pretzel rods
1 (28 oz.) jar	peanut butter, crunchy or creamy
1 pkg.	chocolate almond bark
1 cup	crisp rice cereal, crushed
1 cup	raisins
½ cup	candy sprinkles
1 cup	peanuts, crushed

Spread each pretzel rod with peanut butter and place on foil-lined cookie sheet. In a medium saucepan, melt chocolate almond bark over low heat, stirring often. When melted, spoon evenly over each pretzel rod. Sprinkle pretzels with assorted toppings as desired. Allow to harden on cookie sheet.

Homemade Applesauce

6	red apples
1 cup	water
1 Tbs.	fresh lemon juice
¾ tsp.	cinnamon
¼ cup	sugar

Core and peel all apples, then quarter and cut into chunks. Place apple chunks in a medium saucepan. Add all remaining ingredients and bring to a boil over high heat, stirring often. Reduce heat to medium-low, cover, and simmer for about 20–30 minutes, until apples soften and break apart, stirring every few minutes. Transfer mixture to a food processor and pulse until desired consistency. Serve warm or refrigerate until cooled. Keeps about a week in the refrigerator. Serves 4–6.

Yummy Banana Bread

1⅔ cups	all-purpose flour
2 tsp.	baking powder
½ tsp.	salt
1 tsp.	baking soda
3 med.	very ripe bananas, peeled
⅔ cup	sugar
⅓ cup	vegetable oil
2 lg.	eggs
1½ tsp.	vanilla extract

Preheat oven to 350°F. Grease a 9 x 5 loaf pan with butter or nonstick cooking spray. In a medium bowl, stir together flour, baking powder, salt, and baking soda. In a large bowl, smash the bananas with a fork. Add sugar, oil, eggs, and vanilla, and beat until well blended. Add the flour mixture to the banana mixture. Stir just until blended. Pour batter into prepared loaf pan. Bake for about 45 minutes, until a toothpick inserted into the center of the bread comes out with just a few crumbs clinging to it. Remove pan from oven and cool on a rack for 20 minutes. Gently run a table knife along edges of pan to loosen bread. Carefully turn the loaf out onto a cooling rack. Let cool at least 15 minutes before cutting and serving. Serves 10.

Lemon Blueberry Poppy Seed Bread

1 pkg.	blueberry muffin mix with crumb topping
2 Tbs.	poppy seeds
1	egg
¾ cup	water
½ cup	powdered sugar
1 Tbs.	lemon juice

Preheat oven to 350°F. Spray a loaf pan with nonstick cooking spray. Rinse berries that came in the mix with cold water; drain very well and set aside. Empty muffin mix into medium bowl. Add poppy seeds and stir well to break up any lumps. Add egg and water. Stir until moist, about 50 strokes with a wooden spoon. Fold in berries. Pour gently into loaf pan. Sprinkle with the crumb topping packet from the mix. Bake about 45–55 minutes, until toothpick inserted in the center comes out clean. Cool in pan 10 minutes. Loosen sides of loaf from pan with a table knife. Place a piece of foil over the loaf to keep the topping intact, and flip over onto a plate. Flip again, right side up, onto a cooling rack. Cool completely. Mix powdered sugar and lemon juice together, and drizzle over cooled loaf. Serves 10.

Baked Chicken Nuggets

3	boneless, skinless chicken breasts
1 cup	plain bread crumbs
½ cup	Parmesan cheese, grated
1 tsp.	garlic salt
½ cup	unsalted butter, melted

Preheat oven to 400°F. Line baking sheet with aluminum foil. Cut chicken breast into bite-size chunks. Mix bread crumbs with Parmesan cheese and garlic salt. Dip chicken into melted butter, then roll in crumb mixture. Place on foil-lined baking sheet and bake for 10–12 minutes. Remove from oven and serve warm. Also good cold for leftovers.

Carrot Coins

1 lb.	carrots, peeled and sliced into rounds
1 Tbs.	unsalted butter
2 Tbs.	brown sugar
1 tsp.	water

Place sliced carrots in a microwave-safe bowl and cover with water. Cover bowl loosely with plastic wrap or microwave-safe lid and microwave for 6–7 minutes, until carrots are fork-tender. Drain water and set carrots aside. In a small skillet, melt butter and stir in brown sugar and water. Cook on medium heat for 1 minute. Add carrot coins and toss to coat with brown sugar mixture. Cook on low for 3–4 minutes or until carrots are thoroughly glazed.

Easy Pepperoni Bread

2X

1 (1 lb.) loaf	frozen bread dough, thawed in refrigerator
1 Tbs.	olive oil
½ Tbs.	dried basil
½ Tbs.	dried oregano
8 oz.	sliced pepperoni
1½ cups	mozzarella cheese, shredded
1	egg, lightly beaten
1 tsp.	water

Place dough in a large, lightly greased bowl. Cover and place in a warm location. Allow dough to rise until doubled in size, about two hours, then punch down. Preheat oven to 350°F. Spray a large baking sheet with nonstick cooking spray. Roll dough into a 12 by 18 inch rectangle and brush with olive oil. Sprinkle dough with basil and oregano, then layer with pepperoni, leaving a half-inch border at all edges. Sprinkle with mozzarella cheese. Beginning with the longest edge, roll dough into a thin cylinder and seal seam. Place on baking sheet, seam side down, and brush with egg that has been beaten with 1 teaspoon water. Bake 35 minutes or until golden brown. Slice to serve.

MOPS Favorite: Easiest Chicken Pot Pie

1 (10½ oz.) can	cream of potato soup
1 (29 oz.) can	Homestyle Veg-All, drained
2 cups	chicken, cooked and diced
½ cup	milk
½ tsp.	salt
¼ tsp.	pepper
½ tsp.	dried thyme
2 (9 in.)	pie crusts, unbaked

"Veg-All" is a brand name for a type of canned vegetables containing carrots, celery, potatoes, sweet peas, and onions. The "Homestyle" variety is cut into larger chunks. If you can't find Veg-All in the canned vegetable aisle of your grocery store, you can easily make your own vegetable mixture.

Preheat oven to 375°F. Mix all ingredients together except crusts. Place one crust in the bottom of a deep-dish pie plate. Pour mixture over. Cover with other crust, and crimp edges to seal well. Using a sharp knife, make slits in the top crust to allow steam to escape. Bake 40–45 minutes. Let sit 10 minutes before serving. Serves 4–6.

Kid-Friendly Kabobs

1 lb.	stew beef, cut into 1-inch cubes
3 cups	cherry tomatoes
¼ cup	soy sauce
¼ cup	honey
	salt to taste
4	skewers

If using wooden skewers, make sure to soak them in water for 15 minutes before using so they don't burn.

Preheat oven broiler. Line a baking sheet with foil. Combine beef cubes, cherry tomatoes, soy sauce, honey, and salt in a medium bowl and toss to coat. Alternating, thread beef cubes and tomatoes onto skewers. Place kabobs on baking sheet and broil 10 minutes, turning once.

PB and Apple Sandwiches

2 Tbs.	whipped cream cheese (lighter variety works well)
¼ tsp.	vanilla extract
1 tsp.	honey
1 sm.	tart apple, peeled, cored, and thinly sliced
2 Tbs.	crunchy peanut butter
2 slices	whole wheat bread

Combine cream cheese, vanilla, and honey. Spread cream cheese mixture on one slice of bread. Place apple slices on top. Spread peanut butter on the other slice of bread. Place bread on top of apples, peanut butter side down. Press lightly. Cut in half. Serves 1.

Cheese Sauce for Vegetables

¼ cup	unsalted butter
¼ cup	all-purpose flour
1 tsp.	salt
3 cups	whole milk
2 cups	mild cheddar cheese, shredded

In a medium saucepan, melt butter over medium heat. Add flour and salt, whisking constantly for 2 minutes. Whisk in milk and bring to a boil. Reduce heat to medium-low and simmer for 2 minutes, whisking occasionally. Remove from heat and add cheese. Stir well. Great over all steamed vegetables.

Panko-Crusted Fish Sticks

1 lg.	egg, lightly beaten
⅛ tsp.	salt
⅛ tsp.	black pepper
2 cups	panko (Japanese bread crumbs) or regular bread crumbs
1 Tbs.	seafood seasoning
2 Tbs.	extra virgin olive oil
1½ lbs.	tilapia or whitefish fillets, cut into strips

Preheat oven to 475°F. Spray 1–2 baking sheets with nonstick cooking spray. Place egg in shallow bowl and season with salt and pepper. In a separate bowl, combine panko, seafood seasoning, and olive oil. Toss with a fork to make sure crumbs are evenly coated with oil. Dip fish strips in egg and then in panko mixture. You might need to press with your fingers to make sure crumbs stick. Place on baking sheets, at least an inch apart. Bake without turning until lightly browned, 12–15 minutes.

Cheesy Scrambled Eggs

6 lg.	eggs
¼ cup	milk
1 tsp.	seasoned salt
2 tsp.	unsalted butter
½ cup	cheddar cheese, shredded

Whisk eggs in a small mixing bowl until combined. Add milk and seasoned salt. Whisk again. Melt butter in a nonstick skillet over medium-high heat. Add eggs and cook, stirring constantly, until eggs are barely set, about a minute. Sprinkle with cheese and remove from heat. Let rest a minute while cheese melts. Serve immediately.

Alphabet Soup

2 Tbs.	vegetable oil
2 cups	yellow onion, chopped
1 cup	celery, chopped
1½ cups	carrots, peeled and diced or sliced
2 tsp.	seasoned salt
1	garlic clove, minced
2 qts.	chicken broth
2 cups	water
¼ tsp.	black pepper
1 cup	alphabet pasta, uncooked

Heat oil in a large, heavy stockpot over medium-high heat. Add onion, celery, carrots, and seasoned salt. Cook, stirring frequently, about 5 minutes. Add garlic and cook 2 more minutes. Add broth, water, and pepper. Stir well and bring to a boil. Reduce heat to medium-low and simmer, uncovered, for 30 minutes. Add pasta and stir well. Simmer until pasta is cooked through, about 10 minutes. Serves 8.

Kid's Choice Tater Tot Casserole

1 (32 oz.) bag	frozen tater tots
¼ cup	unsalted butter
1 cup	yellow onion, chopped
1 tsp.	salt
¼ tsp.	black pepper
½ lb.	cooked ham, diced
¼ cup	all-purpose flour
3 cups	milk
3 cups	shredded cheddar cheese

Preheat oven to 425°F. Place tater tots in a 9 x 13 casserole dish. Bake 30 minutes, turning once, until crisp. Reduce heat to 375°F. In a medium saucepan, melt butter over medium heat. Add onion, salt, and pepper. Cook until onion is softened, about 4 minutes, stirring occasionally. Add ham and flour and cook 2 more minutes, stirring constantly. Add milk, still stirring. Bring to a boil. Reduce heat to medium-low and simmer until thickened, about 2 minutes. Stir in 1 cup of the cheese. Pour over tater tots. Top with remaining cheese. Bake until bubbly, about 30 minutes. Let sit 5 minutes before serving.

Egg Salad Pita Pockets

6 lg.	eggs
¼ cup	mayonnaise
¼ tsp.	salt
¼ tsp.	paprika
3	pita rounds, warmed and soft
¼ cup	ranch dressing
1	avocado, pitted and peeled
2 Tbs.	roasted sunflower seeds, shelled

Place eggs in a medium saucepan. Add cold water to cover eggs by 1 inch. Bring to a boil over medium-high heat. Once water is boiling, reduce heat to medium-low. Cook for exactly 10 minutes. Remove saucepan from heat and drain hot water from pan. Run cold water over eggs until they are cool enough to handle. Peel eggs immediately, or it will get much harder once they've cooled. Cut each egg in half, then chop into small pieces. Put chopped eggs in a medium mixing bowl and add mayonnaise, salt, and paprika. Mash with a fork to blend. Store in refrigerator until ready to use. To make pita pockets, cut each pita in half and spread ranch dressing inside each pocket. Cut avocado into 12 thin slices, and place 3 slices inside each pocket. Spoon ¼ cup of the prepared egg salad into each half, and sprinkle with sunflower seeds. Serve immediately. Makes 6.

Two-Cheese Quesadillas

8 (8 in.)	flour tortillas
1 cup	Monterey Jack cheese, grated
1 cup	cheddar cheese, grated
4 tsp.	white onion, finely chopped
4 tsp.	vegetable oil or melted butter
	salsa and guacamole to garnish

Place 1 tortilla on a flat surface. Cover with about ¼ cup of each of the cheeses. Top with 1 teaspoon of onion. Top with another tortilla. Brush top with oil or melted butter. Repeat to make 4 quesadillas. Heat a medium nonstick skillet over medium-low heat. Spray with nonstick cooking spray and place 1 quesadilla in the skillet, ungreased side down. Cook just until golden on the bottom, about 3 minutes. Flip and cook 2 more minutes. Repeat for remaining quesadillas. Serve hot with salsa and guacamole, if desired.

Chinese Fried Rice

2 cups	white rice
4 cups	water
⅔ cup	carrots, diced
½ cup	frozen green peas
2 Tbs.	vegetable oil
¼ cup	green onions, chopped
2	eggs
	soy sauce to taste

To make this a main course, stir in 2 cups leftover cooked pork, chicken, or shrimp.

In a large saucepan, combine rice and water. Bring to a boil. Reduce heat to low. Cover and simmer for 20 minutes. Remove from heat. In a small saucepan, boil carrots in water 3–5 minutes until softened. Add peas and drain. Heat oil in wok or skillet over high heat. Add carrots, peas, and green onion. Cook about 30 seconds. Add eggs, stirring quickly to scramble eggs with vegetables. Stir in cooked rice. Drizzle soy sauce over rice and toss well. Remove from heat. Serves 6–8.

Peanut Blossoms

½ cup	butter-flavored shortening
¾ cup	creamy peanut butter
¾ cup	light brown sugar, firmly packed
½ cup	sugar
1 lg.	egg
2 Tbs.	milk
1 tsp.	vanilla extract
1½ cups	all-purpose flour
1 tsp.	baking soda
½ tsp.	salt
	sugar
48	foil-wrapped milk chocolate pieces, unwrapped

Preheat oven to 375°F. Cream together shortening, peanut butter, brown sugar, and sugar. Add egg, milk, and vanilla. Beat well. Stir together flour, baking soda, and salt. Add to creamed mixture. Beat on low speed until stiff dough forms. Shape into 1-inch balls. Roll each ball in sugar. Place 2 inches apart on ungreased cookie sheet. Bake for 10–12 minutes or until golden brown.

Top each cookie immediately with an unwrapped chocolate piece, pressing down firmly so that cookie cracks around edge. Remove from cookie sheets to cool. Makes 24.

Blackberry Peach Yogurt Popsicles

2 cups	plain Greek yogurt
	honey to taste
½ cup	fresh or frozen blackberries
½ cup	peach or nectarine, chopped

If you choose to add pretzel rods, these popsicles are no longer gluten free.

In a small bowl, sweeten the yogurt with honey to taste. In a blender, purée blackberries and peach or nectarine. Slowly fold the puréed fruit mixture into the yogurt. Pour into 4 popsicle molds or paper cups. If using paper cups, cover each cup with foil. Using a small, sharp knife, make a small slit in the middle of each foil top. Insert popsicle sticks or pretzel rods into foil. Freeze until solid, about 4 hours. When ready to eat, remove popsicles from molds or peel off paper cups. Serve immediately.

Dirt Cups

2 cups	milk
1 (3.9 oz.) pkg.	instant chocolate pudding
8 oz.	whipped topping
16 oz.	Oreo cookies, crushed
8	gummy worms
8	plastic flowers, optional

Pour milk and pudding mix into medium bowl. Whisk until well blended, about 2 minutes. Let stand 5 minutes. Stir in whipped topping and half of crushed cookies. To assemble, place 1 tablespoon crushed cookies in bottom of 8 8-oz. cups. Fill each cup about nearly full with pudding mixture. Top with remaining crumbs. Place gummy worm in "dirt," and a plastic flower in each cup to resemble a flower pot, if desired. Serves 8.

Popcorn Balls

½ cup   molasses
½ cup   light corn syrup
¾ cup   unsalted butter
          salt
8 cups popped popcorn, plain
          butter

In a heavy, medium saucepan, cook molasses with corn syrup until candy thermometer reaches hard crack stage, about 270°F.

Stir in butter and salt to taste. Place popcorn in a large bowl. Slowly stir in the molasses mixture with a wooden spoon, and continue stirring gently until all popcorn is evenly coated. Butter your hands lightly and shape the popcorn into softball-size balls. Set on wax paper and let harden. Wrap with wax paper or plastic wrap to keep fresh.

Peanut Butter Chocolate Crispy Treats

1 cup   sugar
1 cup   light corn syrup
1 cup   peanut butter
6 cups crisp rice cereal
1 cup   semisweet chocolate chips
1 cup   butterscotch morsels

In a medium saucepan, bring sugar and corn syrup to a boil. Add peanut butter and continue to cook, stirring constantly, until well blended. Remove from heat and pour hot mixture over cereal. Mix quickly and thoroughly. Spread into a greased 9 x 13 pan. Quickly sprinkle top with chocolate and butterscotch morsels. Press morsels into bar mixture lightly with back of spoon. Cool, then cut into bars and store at room temperature.

Grasshopper Pie

1 chocolate cookie crust
½ gal. mint chocolate chip ice cream
hot fudge sauce (see recipe p. 252)

Place ice cream in the refrigerator for 10–20 minutes to soften. Spoon softened ice cream into crust, pressing firmly with the back of a spoon. Smooth the top, then place pie in the freezer for about 30 minutes or until firm. When ready to serve, slice pie into 8 pieces and place on individual plates. Drizzle each slice with warm hot fudge sauce. Makes 8 servings.

Chocolate-Dipped Strawberries

1 pint fresh strawberries, washed and dried
1 cup semisweet or bittersweet chocolate chips

Line a baking sheet with parchment or waxed paper. Place chocolate chips in a glass bowl and cover loosely. Microwave on high for 30 seconds. Stir. Continue to microwave in 30-second increments, stirring, until chocolate is melted and smooth. Hold strawberries by the green stem and dip each one into melted chocolate. Place on prepared baking sheet. Refrigerate for 10 minutes to allow chocolate to harden.

MOPS Favorite: Zebra Cake

1 pkg. chocolate cake mix with pudding
8 oz. cream cheese, softened
1 egg
⅓ cup sugar
8 oz. whipped topping, thawed
chocolate syrup, as desired

Prepare cake batter as directed and pour into greased 9 x 13 cake pan. Mix together cream cheese, egg, and sugar. Spoon this mixture randomly onto the cake batter and swirl it with a knife. Bake cake according to package directions. Cool completely. Mix desired amount of chocolate syrup into whipped topping, and spread over cake. Drizzle more syrup over top. Store in refrigerator. Serves 18.

CHAPTER 2

Snacks and Beverages

It's difficult to think anything but pleasant thoughts
while eating a homegrown tomato.

Lewis Grizzard, author and humorist

My first child refused to enter the world on time. He arrived a good three weeks past the date our doctor had estimated, and even then, it was not by his own free will! Hours and hours of hard labor followed by the doctor's decision that I needed a C-section left me exhausted and confused. Things were not going according to my plan! I look back now and laugh at my innocence, as I don't think any part of parenting actually goes as planned. (I think it was Woody Allen who said, "If you want to make God laugh, tell him your plans.")

There was no way I could have known how quickly my exhaustion would be replaced with exhilaration the moment I heard my son's first cry in the operating room late on that September night in 1996. Every ounce of my being responded to his sound, and it felt like a thousand years before I was able to finally hold him close to me and try to bring nourishment to his hungry little body.

If you stop to think about it, the first way a mother shows love to her child centers around food. She nourishes the baby growing inside of her, and she continues to give life even after her baby is born. This is how trust and love begins: the mother gives, the baby trusts, and love is passed between them. What seems like a simple act of feeding another is actually the beginning of one of humanity's most powerful bonds.

Come Lord Jesus, be our guest,
and let these gifts to us be blest. Amen.

Roasted Red Pepper Hummus

2 lg.	garlic cloves, chopped
1 (15 oz.) can	chickpeas (garbanzo beans), drained
⅓ cup	tahini (sesame seed paste)
⅓ cup	freshly squeezed lemon juice
½ cup	roasted red peppers, chopped
	salt and pepper to taste

Mince garlic in a food processor. Scrape down sides and add chick peas, tahini, and lemon juice. Process until smooth. Add roasted peppers and process until desired consistency. I like the peppers finely chopped but not completely puréed. Season with salt and pepper. Serve immediately with pita chips and fresh vegetables, or cover and store in refrigerator up to 1 day. Best served at room temperature. Makes about 2 cups.

Almond Butter Popcorn

¼ cup	unsalted butter
1 cup	light brown sugar
1 cup	almond butter
1 tsp.	salt
8 cups	popped popcorn
1 cup	sliced almonds, toasted, optional

In a medium saucepan, melt butter and add brown sugar, stirring constantly until sugar is dissolved. Remove from heat, stir in almond butter and salt, and mix well. Pour over popcorn and toss to coat evenly. Toss in sliced almonds, if using. Spread on waxed paper to cool.

Orange Cream Popsicles

1 (6 oz.) can	frozen orange juice concentrate, thawed
2 cups	plain yogurt
2 tsp.	vanilla extract
6	small paper cups or popsicle molds
6	popsicle sticks or large pretzel rods

If you do add pretzel rods, these popsicles are no longer gluten free.

Stir orange juice concentrate, yogurt, and vanilla together until smooth. Pour mixture into paper cups or popsicle molds. If using paper cups, cover each cup with foil. Using a small, sharp knife, make a small slit in the middle of each foil top. Insert popsicle sticks or pretzel rods into foil. Freeze cups until solid, about 4 hours. When ready to eat, remove from molds or peel off paper cups. Serve immediately. Serves 6.

Sweet Potato Chips

2 lg.	sweet potatoes, peeled and sliced to about ⅛-inch thick
2 Tbs.	vegetable oil
½ tsp.	salt
¼ tsp.	pepper
¼ tsp.	garlic powder
¼ tsp.	cayenne pepper
¼ tsp.	cumin
½ tsp.	paprika

Preheat oven to 400°F. Toss sweet potato slices with oil in a large bowl. Mix spices together, and toss with potatoes to coat well. On ungreased baking sheets, lay sweet potato slices in a single layer. Bake for 10–12 minutes. Remove from oven and flip sweet potatoes over. Continue baking until golden brown, about 10 more minutes. Keep an eye on them to prevent burning.

Homemade Baked Potato Chips

2 med.	Yukon gold potatoes, peeled and sliced ⅛-inch thick
3 Tbs.	olive or canola oil
	salt and freshly ground pepper to taste

It's crucial to the success of this recipe to slice potatoes extremely thin. Using a mandolin or other handheld slicer will make this much easier.

Preheat oven to 400°F. Toss potato slices in a bowl with oil. Season lightly with salt and pepper, and arrange in a single layer on a baking sheet. Bake until golden brown, about 12–15 minutes, turning once. Season again lightly with salt and pepper when they come out of the oven. Transfer to a rack to cool for maximum crispness.

Pesto Stuffed Mushrooms

2 cups	fresh basil, lightly packed
⅔ cup	olive oil
¼ cup	pine nuts
2	garlic cloves
1 tsp.	salt
½ cup	Parmesan cheese, freshly grated
25	fresh mushrooms, cleaned and stems removed
4–6 oz.	cream cheese

You can purchase ready-made pesto if you're in a hurry. Also, leftover homemade pesto makes a great pizza and pasta sauce.

For the pesto, purée basil, olive oil, pine nuts, garlic, and salt in a food processor until smooth. Stir in Parmesan cheese. Refrigerate if not using immediately. When ready, fill each mushroom cap with cream cheese. Top with a small dollop of pesto. Heat under oven broiler until bubbly.

Warm Cheesy Bean Dip

3 cups	canned black beans, drained
½ cup	white onion, chopped
2	garlic cloves, chopped
10	pickled jalapeño slices
1 Tbs.	lemon juice
¼ tsp.	salt
2 Tbs.	unsalted butter, melted
2 cups	white cheddar cheese, shredded
1 Tbs.	milk

I often make this with black-eyed peas instead of black beans.

Purée beans in food processor with onion, garlic, and jalapeño. Stir in lemon juice, salt, and butter. In a medium saucepan over low heat, melt cheese into beans, stirring often. Add milk, and stir until thoroughly combined. Serve warm with corn chips. Serves 8.

MOPS Mom: Cheese Fondue

Heidi Johnson, Wake Forest, North Carolina

2 Tbs.	unsalted butter
2 Tbs.	all-purpose flour
1 cup	milk
1 cup	Swiss cheese, shredded
½ tsp.	garlic powder
dash	pepper
	French or sourdough bread, cubed
	assorted vegetables

Melt butter in microwave in a medium microwave-safe bowl. Blend flour into the melted butter. Whisk in milk. Mixture will look somewhat lumpy. Cover and heat in microwave on high for 2–3 minutes until it starts to thicken. Stir until smooth. Heat in microwave for another 2 minutes, until thickened. If the mixture isn't thickened, microwave for another 2 minutes. Add Swiss cheese, garlic powder, and pepper, and stir until cheese has melted. Serve warm with bread and vegetables for dipping.

Sweet Onion Dip

1 lg.	sweet yellow onion, coarsely chopped
1½ cups	reduced fat mayonnaise
½ cup	Swiss cheese, shredded
½ cup	Parmesan cheese, grated
	paprika to garnish

Preheat oven to 350°F. Place onion in a food processor and pulse until very finely chopped. Add mayonnaise and cheeses and pulse to blend. Spread in a 9-inch pie plate or 8 x 8 baking dish and sprinkle with paprika. Bake for 30 minutes until spread is bubbly and top is golden. Serve with crackers, pita chips, or plain potato chips.

Easiest Chinese Chicken Lettuce Wraps

1	rotisserie chicken, preferably teriyaki-seasoned
1 Tbs.	sesame or canola oil
¼ cup	red bell pepper, diced
¼ cup	water chestnuts, diced
¼ cup	bamboo shoots, diced
2 Tbs.	green onion, thinly sliced
2 Tbs.	soy sauce
1 tsp.	fresh ginger, minced
2	garlic cloves, minced
8–12	lettuce leaves, depending on size
½ cup	cashews, chopped and toasted, optional

Remove meat from rotisserie chicken, about 3 cups, and chop fine. Heat oil in a large skillet over medium-high heat. Add red pepper, water chestnuts, bamboo shoots, and green onion. Cook until heated through, about 5 minutes. Add chicken, soy sauce, ginger, and garlic. Mix well and remove from heat. Serve with lettuce leaves for wrapping, and sprinkle with toasted cashews, if desired.

Autumn Pumpkin Dip

6 oz.	cream cheese, softened
½ cup	light brown sugar
½ cup	canned pumpkin purée
2 tsp.	maple syrup
½ tsp.	cinnamon

Beat cream cheese and sugar together until well blended. Add remaining ingredients and stir to combine. Serve with sliced apples and pears. Store in refrigerator.

Wasabi Nuts and Bolts

2 cups	unsalted mixed nuts
1 tsp.	onion powder
1 tsp.	garlic powder
2 tsp.	smoked paprika
½ tsp.	salt
1 (3.5 oz.) bag	microwave popcorn
2 cups	wasabi peas
2 cups	cheese snack crackers
2 cups	pretzel sticks or snaps

Preheat oven to 350°F. Line a baking sheet with foil. Spread nuts on baking sheet and lightly coat with cooking spray. In a small bowl, mix together onion powder, garlic powder, smoked paprika, and salt. Sprinkle 1 teaspoon over nuts. Bake for 8 minutes.

Meanwhile, microwave popcorn according to package directions. Immediately place popcorn in a large bowl and sprinkle with remaining spice mixture. Toss to coat. Add toasted nuts, wasabi peas, cheese snack crackers, and pretzel sticks. Toss to combine. Store in airtight container.

Chocolate Hazelnut Fruit Dip

3 Tbs.	chocolate hazelnut spread, such as Nutella
3 Tbs.	cream cheese, softened
	pinch of salt
¼ cup	milk

Blend together chocolate hazelnut spread, cream cheese, and salt. Slowly stir in milk a little at a time until you reach a creamy consistency. Serve immediately or store in refrigerator. Dip will harden in refrigerator, so microwave for 10–15 seconds and stir before serving. Makes ½ cup.

Zucchini Squares

3 cups	zucchini, unpeeled and thinly sliced
1 cup	biscuit mix
½ cup	yellow onion, finely chopped
¼ tsp.	dried oregano
¼ tsp.	black pepper
½ tsp.	salt, or to taste
dash	garlic powder
½ cup	Parmesan cheese, grated
¼ cup	vegetable oil
4	eggs, lightly beaten

Combine all ingredients in a large bowl; mix well. Pour mixture into a 9 x 13 baking dish that has been sprayed with nonstick cooking spray. Bake at 350°F for about 30 minutes or until lightly browned. Let cool slightly before cutting into squares for an appetizer. Makes 24 small squares.

White Bean Dip

1 (15 oz.) can	white beans, drained and rinsed
3 Tbs.	olive oil
3 Tbs.	lemon juice
¼ tsp.	salt
¼ tsp.	freshly ground black pepper

This is also delicious served warm. Place in microwaveable bowl and heat in microwave on medium heat for 30 seconds. Stir. Heat for 30 more seconds.

Place beans, oil, lemon juice, salt, and pepper in food processor or blender. Process until smooth. Add more salt and pepper to taste, if you like. Serve cold or at room temperature with pita chips or carrot sticks. Makes 1½ cups. Stores in refrigerator up to 3 days.

MOPS Mom: Warm Bacon Cheese Spread

■ *Tricia Marble, Homosassa, Florida* ■

Tricia Marble's father found this recipe for Warm Bacon Cheese Spread and made it one year for their family's annual Christmas gathering at his house. "There are three girls in my family, and we all gather at his house for Christmas," Tricia said. "We make the most out of Christmas memories because our mom passed away last year at the young age of sixty-three from a form of Alzheimer's disease."

The dip has become the most-requested recipe every time friends and family get together.

Tricia learned to cook through what she calls "Hit and miss with LOTS of misses!" She and her husband, Peter, have two boys. "MOPS was a lifesaver for me when my boys were little," Tricia said. "Life was often overwhelming with no family in the area and a husband who worked long hours. MOPS taught me that I wasn't alone. It brought me hope, and I made friends that have stayed with me through this journey as my children grow older."

1 (1 lb.) loaf	round sourdough bread
8 oz.	cream cheese, softened
1½ cups	sour cream
2 cups	cheddar cheese, shredded
1½ tsp.	Worcestershire sauce
¾ lb.	bacon, cooked and crumbled
½ cup	chopped green onions
	assorted crackers

Cut the top quarter off of loaf of bread. Carefully hollow out remaining loaf, leaving a 1-inch-thick shell. Cut removed bread and top of loaf into cubes; set aside. In a mixing bowl, beat the cream cheese until creamy. Add sour cream, cheddar cheese, and Worcestershire sauce. Stir until combined. Stir in bacon and onions. Spoon dip into bread shell. Wrap in heavy duty foil. Bake at 325°F for 1 hour or until heated through. Serve with crackers and reserved bread cubes. Makes 4 cups.

MOPS Mom: My Grandmother's Artichoke Dip

■ *Angela Marie McGillicuddy Stacey, Eureka, California* ■

In Loving Memory of Joyce Hubler

"My grandmother was my everything," Angela shared. "She was my mom, grandmother, friend, and confidante all wrapped into one. She was from Texas and everything she did was big! It is an honor to be able to share her recipes."

2 (14 oz.) cans	artichoke hearts, drained
4 oz.	diced pimentos, drained
2 bunches	green onions, chopped
1 cup	mayonnaise
1 cup	cheddar cheese, shredded
1½ cups	Parmesan cheese, shredded

Preheat oven to 350°F. Mix together artichoke hearts, pimentos, green onions, mayonnaise, and cheddar cheese. Spoon into a greased, square casserole dish. Top with Parmesan cheese. Bake until bubbly, about 30 minutes. Serve with assorted crackers and pita chips. Makes 10–12 party servings.

MOPS Favorite: Vegetable Pizza

2 pkgs.	refrigerated crescent rolls
8 oz.	cream cheese, softened
1 cup	cottage cheese
¾ cup	mayonnaise
1 pkg.	dry ranch dressing mix
½–1 cup each	broccoli, cauliflower, onions, bell peppers, carrots, fresh mushrooms, and tomatoes, finely chopped

Place rolls flat on greased cookie sheet, pressing together all perforated edges. Bake according to package directions. Cool. Mix together cheeses, mayonnaise, and dressing mix. Spread over cooled crust. Sprinkle with chopped vegetables, putting tomatoes on last. Cut into squares. Makes 64 squares.

MOPS Favorite: Puppy Chow

1 cup	peanut butter
1 cup	chocolate chips
½ cup	unsalted butter
8 cups	Chex cereal, any flavor
2 cups	powdered sugar

Melt peanut butter, chocolate chips, and butter together in microwave on high for 2 minutes. Stir to combine. Place cereal in brown paper grocery bag, and pour peanut butter mixture over. Shake well until thoroughly combined. Add powdered sugar; shake well to coat. Store in an airtight container. Serves 12.

Roasted Corn Guacamole

2 Tbs.	corn oil
2 cups	frozen corn kernels, thawed
2 cups	purchased or prepared guacamole
¼ tsp.	cumin
	salt to taste

Preheat oven to 450°F. Drizzle corn oil on a baking sheet and add corn, spreading evenly. Roast for 8 minutes. Transfer to a mixing bowl. Add guacamole, cumin, and salt to taste and mix gently but thoroughly. Cover tightly and chill until serving time. Serve with corn tortilla chips.

Classic Italian Bruschetta

1½ lbs.	ripe plum tomatoes
6–8	garlic cloves, minced
1 med.	shallot, minced
1 cup	fresh basil leaves, packed
½ tsp.	salt
½ tsp.	freshly ground black pepper
1 tsp.	fresh lemon juice
¼ cup	olive oil
1	French baguette

Dice tomatoes to ¼ inch and add to a large bowl with minced garlic and shallot, and toss. Coarsely chop basil leaves and add to the bowl with salt, pepper, lemon juice, and olive oil. Toss again. Let stand at room temperature for at least 30 minutes and up to 4 hours. Serve with slices of baguette.

Tortellini Skewers

1 lb.	cheese tortellini, cooked and rinsed
½ cup	vinaigrette dressing of your choice
1	red or yellow bell pepper, cut into 1-inch pieces
1 pint	cherry or grape tomatoes
10 (6 inch)	skewers

Kids love making these skewers—which makes them more likely to eat those vegetables.

In a large bowl, pour vinaigrette dressing over cooked tortellini and gently toss. Let sit 30 minutes. On each skewer, thread tortellini, bell pepper, and tomatoes. If desired, serve with additional dressing to dip.

Peacho De Gallo

4	fresh, ripe peaches, peeled, pitted, and finely chopped
¼ cup	red onion, finely chopped
1	jalapeño pepper, seeded and finely chopped
1 Tbs.	fresh cilantro, chopped
1 tsp.	fresh lime juice
	sea salt to taste

To add more heat, leave the seeds in the jalapeño pepper.

Combine all ingredients in a medium bowl. Let stand at room temperature for at least 30 minutes to allow flavors to develop. Make up to 1 day in advance. Keep refrigerated. Great with tortilla chips, or as a topping for grilled shrimp or chicken.

Black Bean and Corn Salsa

2 (15 oz.) cans	black beans, drained and rinsed
1 (16 oz.) can	white corn, drained
½ cup	fresh cilantro, finely chopped
¼ cup	green onions, finely chopped
⅓ cup	fresh lime juice
3 Tbs.	olive oil
1 Tbs.	ground cumin
½ tsp.	salt, or to taste
1 (4 oz.) can	chopped green chiles, drained
3 dashes	hot pepper sauce, optional

Combine all ingredients. Mix well and refrigerate until ready to serve, up to 1 day in advance. Serve with corn chips or over grilled chicken.

Jalapeño Cranberry Salsa

3 cups	fresh cranberries
½ med.	red onion, quartered
2	jalapeño peppers, seeded and halved (use less for milder flavor)
½ cup	fresh cilantro, chopped
½ cup	honey
2 Tbs.	fresh lime juice
dash	kosher salt

Place all ingredients in food processor. Pulse 8 times or until coarsely chopped. Scrape sides of bowl midway through pulses. Cover and chill at least 8 hours. Perfect with sweet potato chips or as a holiday relish with turkey and dressing.

Spicy Edamame Guacamole

1 cup	frozen shelled edamame, thawed
1	ripe avocado, peeled and pitted
1	canned chipotle pepper in adobo sauce, finely chopped
⅓ cup	fresh cilantro, finely chopped
½ cup	white onion, chopped
2 Tbs.	fresh lime juice
2 Tbs.	water
	salt and pepper to taste

Store leftover canned chipotle peppers in small, individual plastic bags and freeze—then pull out and use as needed.

Put edamame, avocado, chipotle, cilantro, onion, and lime juice in food processor and pulse until almost smooth. Add enough water to make consistency creamy and pulse again. Transfer guacamole to a bowl, season with salt and pepper, and serve. Great with pita chips and vegetable sticks.

Prosciutto Pinwheels

1 (17.5 oz.) box	frozen puff pastry (2 sheets), thawed
⅔ cup	Dijon mustard, divided
¾ lb.	prosciutto, shredded and divided
2 cups	provolone cheese, shredded, divided

Preheat oven to 425°F. Grease large baking sheet. Working with 1 sheet of puff pastry, keeping remaining sheet wrapped and cold, roll out on lightly floured surface to 14 inches square. Brush with thin layer of mustard. Cover with half of the prosciutto slices, slightly overlapping and leaving ½ inch border around edges. Sprinkle with 1 cup cheese. Roll pastry tightly. Pinch seams to seal and tuck ends under. Repeat with remaining pastry sheet. Cut into ½-inch slices and place, cut side up, 1 inch apart on prepared baking sheet. Bake 10–15 minutes without turning, until golden brown.

Tex-Mex Cheese Steak Nachos

1 Tbs.	vegetable oil
1 cup	poblano pepper, chopped
1 cup	white onion, chopped
6 oz.	sirloin, flank, or rib eye steak, cubed
	salt and pepper
1 (16 oz.) can	refried beans
6 oz.	large, sturdy tortilla chips
1 cup	cheddar cheese, shredded
	sour cream, diced tomato, guacamole, or chopped jalepeño pepper to garnish

Heat oil in a large skillet over medium-high heat. Add peppers and onions and sauté for about 4 minutes, until tender. Remove from skillet and set aside. Sprinkle steak with salt and pepper. Add to skillet and cook over medium-high heat until browned but still medium-rare, about 4 minutes. Remove from heat. Heat refried beans in microwave until warmed throughout, about 2 minutes, stirring once. Preheat oven broiler. Arrange tortilla chips on baking sheet and top each with a dollop of refried beans, a cube of steak, and a sprinkle of peppers and onions. Sprinkle with shredded cheese. Broil, watching carefully, until cheese melts. Remove from oven and garnish as desired with sour cream, diced tomato, guacamole, and/or chopped jalepeño pepper. Serve immediately.

Frozen Peach Lemonade

	ice cubes
6 oz.	frozen pink lemonade concentrate
6 oz.	club soda or lemon-lime carbonated soda
2 med.	ripe peaches, pitted and halved but not peeled

Fill blender half-full with ice cubes. Add frozen pink lemonade concentrate, soda, and peach halves. Blend until smooth.

Sparkling Pink Lemonade

2 (12 oz.) cans	frozen pink lemonade concentrate, thawed
1 gal.	chilled club soda

Combine lemonade concentrate and club soda just before serving. Stir well to blend. Makes 35 4-oz. servings.

Fruity Iced Tea

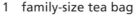

1	family-size tea bag
1 (6 oz.) can	frozen pink lemonade concentrate, thawed
1 cup	sugar
1 cup	pineapple juice

Bring a medium saucepan of water to a boil. Add tea bag and steep for 20 minutes. In a 1 gallon pitcher, add pink lemonade concentrate, sugar, and pineapple juice. Mix well and add tea. Add additional cold water to make one gallon. Serve cold.

Strawberry Lemonade

2 pints	fresh strawberries, washed, hulled, and patted dry
1 cup + 4 tsp.	sugar, divided
1 cup	freshly squeezed lemon juice
	club soda

Purée 1 pint strawberries with 2 teaspoons sugar in a blender. Repeat with remaining pint of strawberries and 2 teaspoons sugar. Set out 4 8-oz. glasses, and spoon 3 tablespoons strawberry purée, ¼ cup sugar, and ¼ cup lemon juice into each glass. Stir, and add ice. Top off glasses with club soda. Add more sugar, if desired.

Old-Fashioned Citrus Tea

10	regular-size tea bags
6 cups	water
1½ cups	sugar
1 (6 oz.) can	frozen lemonade concentrate, thawed
1 (6 oz.) can	frozen orange juice concentrate, thawed

Bring water to a boil. Brew tea bags for approximately 15 minutes. Discard tea bags. Mix sugar, lemonade concentrate, and orange juice concentrate with tea. Stir well until combined. Pour into 1 gallon pitcher and add cold water to make 1 gallon. Stir well. Serve cold.

Watermelon Lemonade

½ cup	freshly squeezed lemon juice
2 cups	seedless watermelon chunks
6 Tbs.	simple syrup
1½ cups	water

Place chunks of seeded watermelon in blender and blend until smooth; there should be about 1 cup purée. For simple syrup, mix 6 tablespoons sugar with 6 tablespoons water, and heat in microwave until sugar is dissolved. Mix lemon juice, purée, syrup, and water in a small pitcher. Store in refrigerator and pour over ice to serve. Makes 4 small servings.

White Hot Chocolate

1 cup	white chocolate chips
1 cup	heavy cream
4 cups	milk
1 tsp.	vanilla extract

Garnish with whipped cream and chocolate shavings, if desired.

Heat white chocolate chips and heavy cream together in a saucepan over medium heat, stirring continuously, until white chocolate chips are melted. Stir in milk and vanilla, and heat through. Pour into mugs and serve immediately.

CHAPTER 3

Breakfast

I know that young children will wander away from the table, and that family life is never smooth, and that life itself is full, not only of charm and warmth and comfort but of sorrow and tears. But whether we are happy or sad, we must be fed. Both happy and sad people can be cheered up by a nice meal.

Laurie Colwin, Home Cooking

Our senses are a tremendous gift in helping us remember what is beautiful.

My childhood home had its own set of comforting sounds and smells. I think all of our homes have their unique soundtracks too, but we don't really notice them because we're so busy running through our days and nights.

Now that I'm older and have gone back home for visits, these familiarities have been a source of pleasure to rediscover.

From where my childhood bedroom is upstairs, I could always hear the early morning sounds of my parents at the breakfast table. I couldn't hear words, just the calm rhythm of conversation and coffee cups. I returned home again the other day for a visit, and was awakened from a sound sleep in my old bedroom when the morning sun came through my window. I wasn't fully coherent as I heard my parents talking at the breakfast table, just like they did decades ago. For a split second I thought I was ten years old again, safe at home.

And the smells! Fried chicken. Peach cobbler. Corn bread. From my earliest memories of baking biscuits with my mother to crowding around our table laughing with all of my aunts, uncles, and cousins, I loved being at home, especially at mealtimes.

Home and food: two earthly necessities that are so ordinary for most of us we don't really think about them much. But one thing I've noticed in my life is that God most often speaks to me through the ordinary. In fact, when God chose to come to earth, he arrived in a body like ours. He didn't wow us with answers to the mysteries of the universe. He showed up in the places where he knew we needed him the most. He came into our homes and reminded us he was going to take us home with him one day. He ate with us at our tables and explained that he was the bread and wine of our lives, fulfilling the hunger in each of us to know security, unconditional love, contentment, and peace.

Home and food. The gifts of this earth suddenly seem extraordinarily beautiful.

Father, we thank thee for the night,
And for the pleasant morning light.
For rest and food and loving care,
And all that makes the day so fair.
Help us to do the thing we should,
To be to others kind and good,
In all we do, in all we say,
To grow more loving every day.

Blueberry Biscuits with Lemon Glaze

For the biscuits:

3 cups	biscuit baking mix
¼ cup	sugar
1 cup	milk
1 cup	fresh or frozen blueberries

For the glaze:

½ cup	sifted powdered sugar
1 Tbs.	lemon juice

Preheat oven to 400°F and spray a baking sheet with nonstick cooking spray. In a large bowl, combine baking mix and sugar. Stir milk into dry ingredients just until moistened. Fold in blueberries gently. If using frozen berries, do not thaw them first or biscuits will turn blue.

Turn dough out gently on a lightly floured surface. Pat to ¾-inch thick and cut with 2-inch cutter—but don't twist the cutter. The biscuits won't rise as high. Place biscuits 1 inch apart on prepared baking sheet. Bake for 11–13 minutes, until lightly browned. Meanwhile, combine glaze ingredients. When biscuits have cooled slightly, drizzle with glaze. Makes 10–12 biscuits.

Restaurant-Style Biscuits

8 oz.	sour cream
1 cup	club soda, divided
4½ cups	biscuit baking mix, divided
¼ cup	unsalted butter, melted

Preheat oven to 450°F. Mix sour cream with half of the club soda. Add 4 cups biscuit mix. Stir with a spoon until just blended. Add remaining club soda and stir again until just blended. (Overstirring will make the biscuits tough.) On a lightly floured surface, pat the dough out to about 1-inch thick. You will need the remaining ½ cup of biscuit mix to keep the dough from being too sticky. Cut with a large biscuit cutter, but don't twist while cutting or the biscuits won't rise as high. Place on a baking sheet and brush with melted butter. Bake for 15 minutes, or until lightly browned.

Orange Rolls

½ cup	sugar
1½ tsp.	grated orange rind
½ tsp.	cinnamon
1 (12 oz.) can	refrigerated buttermilk biscuits
3 Tbs.	orange juice

Preheat oven to 350°F. Spray a 9-inch round cake pan with nonstick cooking spray. Combine first 3 ingredients. Dip each biscuit in orange juice, then dredge in sugar mixture. Arrange biscuits in prepared pan. Sprinkle with remaining sugar mixture and drizzle with orange juice. Bake for 25 minutes or until golden brown. Serve warm. Makes 10 orange rolls.

No-Rise Cinnamon Rolls

For the cinnamon sugar filling:

¼ cup	brown sugar
2 tsp.	cinnamon

For the dough:

2½ cups	all-purpose flour
2 Tbs.	brown sugar, packed
2 tsp.	baking powder
½ tsp.	salt
1½ cups + 1 Tbs.	heavy cream or milk (cream makes richer rolls)

For the icing:

6 Tbs.	powdered sugar
4–6 tsp.	milk

Preheat oven to 400°F. For filling, combine brown sugar and cinnamon in a small bowl. Set aside. For dough, in a large bowl stir together flour, brown sugar, baking powder, and salt. Add 1½ cups cream or milk, and stir until the dough forms a ball, about 1 minute. With your hands, fold the dough over a few times in the bowl, until dough is smooth. Turn the dough out onto a lightly floured surface. Pat dough into a ½-inch thick rectangle, about 9 by 13 inches. Brush the surface of the dough with the remaining tablespoon of cream. Sprinkle evenly with the cinnamon sugar topping. Starting from the long side, roll the dough into a cylinder. Slice into 9 equal rounds. Place the rounds, cut side down, into an ungreased square baking dish or a pie plate. Bake for about 30 minutes, until rolls are lightly browned. For icing, mix together powdered sugar and milk until smooth. When you remove rolls from the oven, immediately drizzle with icing. Serve warm. Makes 9.

Miniature Banana Cinnamon Muffins

½ cup	ripe bananas
¾ cup	plain yogurt
1 tsp.	vanilla extract
1½ cups	all-purpose flour
1½ tsp.	baking powder
¼ tsp.	baking soda
¼ tsp.	salt
5 Tbs.	unsalted butter, softened
½ cup	sugar
1 lg.	egg
¾ cup	cinnamon chips

Preheat oven to 425°F. Line 24 miniature muffin cups with muffin liners or spray with nonstick cooking spray. Using a fork, mash banana, yogurt, and vanilla together in a small bowl.

In a separate bowl, mix together flour, baking powder, baking soda, and salt, and set aside. Cream butter and sugar together using an electric mixer. Add egg and combine until smooth. Reduce speed to low and, alternating, add dry ingredients and banana mixture, beginning and ending with dry ingredients. Beat until batter is just smooth, then mix batter on high for about 30 seconds. Gently stir in cinnamon chips with a wooden spoon. Completely fill each muffin cup with batter and bake until golden brown, about 12–14 minutes. Let cool 3 minutes on a wire rack, then remove muffins from tins and invert on rack to cool completely.

MOPS Favorite: Chocolate Chip Muffins

1½ cups	all-purpose flour
½ cup	sugar
1 Tbs.	baking powder
¼ tsp.	salt
1 cup	chocolate chips
⅓ cup	unsalted butter
1	egg
1 cup	milk

Preheat oven to 375°F. Mix dry ingredients together. Add chocolate chips. In microwave, melt butter in glass measuring cup. Cool. Mix in egg and milk, but do not beat. Stir gently into flour mixture. Pour into greased or paper-lined muffin tins. Bake 20–25 minutes. Makes 12 muffins.

Blueberry Oatmeal Muffins

1⅔ cups	quick-cooking oats
⅔ cup	all-purpose flour
½ cup	whole wheat flour
¾ cup	light brown sugar, packed
2 tsp.	cinnamon
1 tsp.	baking powder
1 tsp.	baking soda
¾ tsp.	salt
1½ cups	low fat buttermilk
¼ cup	oil
2 lg.	eggs (or 3 egg whites)
⅓ cup	low fat plain yogurt
2 cups	blueberries, washed and completely dry
2 Tbs.	sugar
2 Tbs.	oats

These muffins are not as sweet as other muffins, but they are delicious!

Preheat oven to 400°F. Place oats in a food processor; pulse 5–6 times or until oats resemble coarse meal. Place in a large bowl. Add flours, brown sugar, cinnamon, baking powder, baking soda, and salt. Stir well. Combine buttermilk, oil, eggs, and yogurt in a separate bowl. Add to flour mixture and stir gently just until moist. Gently fold in blueberries. Spoon batter into 12 muffin cups (or 6 jumbo cups) coated with nonstick cooking spray. Mix together 2 tablespoons sugar and 2 tablespoons oats and sprinkle evenly over muffins. Bake for 20 minutes or until muffins spring back when touched lightly in center. Remove from pans immediately; place on a wire rack to cool.

MOPS Mom: Easiest Muffins You'll Ever Make

■ *Lindsey Bell, Carterville, Missouri* ■

Lindsey Bell has a Bible verse that appears at the bottom of her emails: Colossians 3:23. "Whatever you do, work at it with all your heart, as working for the Lord, not for men." As a mother of one young son, Rylan, and a wife to her husband, Keith, Lindsey keeps this verse at the front of her mind as she works throughout the day to take care of her home and family. She and Keith have not had an easy year and have had to suffer through some serious trauma, but still, Lindsey remains a faithful and loving wife and mother. This recipe is one of her family's favorites, and so easy to make!

| 1 pkg. | spice or chocolate cake mix |
| 1 (15 oz.) can | pumpkin purée |

Preheat oven to 350°F. Mix together cake mix and pumpkin purée. Spoon into greased muffin tins. Bake for 15–20 minutes or until toothpick inserted in center comes out clean. Makes 12 muffins.

Pecan Pie Muffins

1 cup	light brown sugar, packed
½ cup	all-purpose flour
1 cup	pecans, chopped
⅔ cup	unsalted butter, melted
2	eggs, beaten
½ tsp.	vanilla extract

These are perfect as miniature muffins too. Recipe will make about 32 miniature muffins. Reduce cooking time to 12–15 minutes.

Preheat oven to 350°F. Spray a 12-count muffin tin with nonstick cooking spray or use liners. Combine brown sugar, flour, and pecans in a bowl. Set aside. In another bowl, mix together butter, eggs, and vanilla. Add to the flour mixture and stir just until moistened. Fill each muffin cup ¾ full. Bake for 20–25 minutes.

Six-Week Bran Muffins

4	eggs
3 cups	sugar
1 qt.	buttermilk
6 cups	bran flake cereal (with or without raisins)
5 cups	all-purpose flour
1 cup	vegetable oil
5 tsp.	baking soda
1 tsp.	salt

If you don't like raisins, use plain bran flakes and add 1 cup dried fruit of your choice. I love dried cranberries in mine.

In a large bowl, beat eggs and sugar until well combined. Stir in buttermilk, cereal, flour, oil, baking soda, and salt; mix well. Refrigerate batter at least 6 hours before using the first time. When ready to bake, fill greased or paper-lined muffin cups ⅔ full. Bake at 400°F for 15–20 minutes or until a toothpick inserted near the center comes out clean. Batter may be stored, covered, in the refrigerator for up to 6 weeks. Makes 4 dozen muffins.

Chocolate Chip Croissants

1 (8 ct.) tube	refrigerated crescent rolls
⅓ cup	miniature semisweet chocolate chips
1	egg, beaten with 1 tsp. water

Heat oven to 375°F. Unroll the refrigerated dough and separate it into 8 triangles. Place about 10 chocolate chips on the bottom third of each triangle and roll the dough up around the chocolate. Transfer the croissants to a baking sheet lined with parchment paper. Brush lightly with egg wash. Bake until golden brown, 12–14 minutes. Serve warm or at room temperature. Makes 8.

Plucking Bread

2 doz.	frozen rolls, thawed
¾ cup	unsalted butter, melted
1½ cups	sugar
¾ tsp.	cinnamon
	chopped pecans, optional

You can use canned biscuits instead of roll dough and skip the rising step.

Cut each roll in 3 pieces. I use kitchen scissors to make it easier. Mix sugar and cinnamon together in a small bowl. Dip each roll in melted butter and then the sugar mixture. Layer rolls in an ungreased tube or Bundt pan. Sprinkle with pecans, if desired. Let rise about 2 hours, covered loosely with a damp tea towel. Bake on bottom rack of 350°F oven for 40 minutes.

Delicious Glazed Cranberry Bread

For the bread:

2 cups	all-purpose flour
1 cup	sugar
1½ tsp.	baking powder
1 tsp.	salt
½ tsp.	baking soda
¼ cup	unsalted butter
1	egg, beaten
¾ cup	orange juice
1 tsp.	orange zest
1½ cups	fresh cranberries

Doubling this recipe makes a great Bundt-style cake. Increase cooking time to 75 minutes, checking often. Cake is done when a toothpick inserted in center comes out clean.

For the glaze:

2 cups	sifted powdered sugar
¼ cup	unsalted butter, softened
½ tsp.	vanilla extract
	milk, for thinning glaze

Preheat oven to 350°F. Grease and flour a loaf pan. For the bread, sift dry ingredients together. Cut butter into dry ingredients with 2 knives or a pastry blender, or by pulsing with a food processor, until mixture resembles coarse crumbs. Combine egg, orange juice, and zest, and mix into flour mixture. Stir cranberries gently into batter. Bake for 45–55 minutes, until toothpick inserted in center comes out clean. Remove loaf from oven and let cool 10 minutes in pan before turning out on a wire rack to cool completely. To glaze, mix together powdered sugar, butter, vanilla, and enough milk to make a fairly thick glaze and drizzle over the bread. Let glaze harden a bit before covering the loaf with foil.

MOPS Mom: Hearty Pancakes

■ *Marie Riley, Shawnee, Kansas* ■

Marie Riley has served on the steering team for her local MOPS for two years. "Being a mom can feel so isolating. I love bringing a new mom into our MOPS group because she is bound to find someone she can identify with. I love the great friendships that form!" Marie said. Marie's kids love pancakes, but she wanted them to have healthier ones that still tasted great. "I nixed the butter for canola oil and applesauce, cut the sugar in half, and doubled the oats, and my kids still gobbled them up," Marie added. "I sometimes add a sprinkling of chocolate chips and then they don't need syrup."

For the dry ingredients:

1 cup	whole wheat flour
¾ cup	all-purpose flour
½ cup	rolled oats, old-fashioned or quick-cooking
1 tsp.	salt
2 Tbs.	sugar
½ tsp.	cinnamon
½ tsp.	baking soda
2 tsp.	baking powder

For the wet ingredients:

1¾ cups	milk
3	eggs
2 Tbs.	canola oil
2 Tbs.	applesauce
1 tsp.	vanilla extract

In a large bowl, whisk together all of the dry ingredients. In another bowl, whisk together the wet ingredients. Pour the wet ingredients over the dry ingredients and stir together until combined, but do not overmix. Preheat a griddle to medium-high heat. Cook pancakes in ¼-cup batches or whatever size your family prefers. Serves 4.

MOPS Favorite: Family Pancakes

2	eggs
1 cup	sour cream
2 cups	milk
2½ cups	baking mix, such as Pioneer
2 Tbs.	unsalted butter, melted
½ tsp.	vanilla extract

Try sprinkling berries, chocolate chips, or chopped nuts on each pancake just before flipping!

Beat eggs in a large bowl. Blend in sour cream. Stir in milk. Add baking mix and beat with a wire whisk just until smooth. Stir in melted butter and vanilla. Cook pancakes on a large griddle or nonstick skillet over medium-high heat until lightly golden and no longer runny in the center. (It's time to flip the pancake when the surface is bubbly.) Serve with your favorite syrup. Makes 20 4-inch pancakes.

Bananas Foster French Toast

For the toast:

6	eggs
2 cups	half-and-half (can use fat free)
½ cup	sugar
2 tsp.	cinnamon
1 tsp.	vanilla extract
½ cup	unsalted butter
1 loaf	French bread, sliced diagonally about 1½ in. thick

This sauce is also delicious over ice cream, pound cake, and anything else you can imagine!

For the sauce:

½ cup	unsalted butter
4 cups	bananas, sliced
2 tsp.	vanilla extract
¾ cup	pecan or walnut pieces
1½ cups	maple syrup

Preheat oven to 225°F. Combine all ingredients for the French toast except bread and butter and stir well. Soak bread in batter for 5 minutes, turning once to soak both sides evenly. Heat butter over medium heat in a large skillet. Brown soaked bread on each side and place in baking dish. Keep French toast warm in oven until all slices are cooked.

For sauce, add butter and bananas to same pan. Cook 5 minutes. Add vanilla. Stir in pecans and syrup. Remove French toast from oven and top with sauce. Serve immediately. Serves 6–8.

MOPS Mom: Overnight Caramel French Toast

■ *Sarah Clark, Crossroads MOPS, Raleigh, North Carolina* ■

Sarah Clark grew up in a home with a mom who cooked a lot, so Sarah followed in her footsteps . . . although she admits she still had much to learn when she married her husband, Michael. Sarah was new in town with one toddler when she was first invited to MOPS by a fellow Marine wife. "My MOPS friends have been there with me through three moves, a deployment, and more children," Sarah said. "Through being a part of MOPS I have also discovered many things about myself and many interests I never knew I had. MOPS has given me the opportunity to love and serve other moms, something I will be forever grateful for!" Sarah and Michael are the parents of Gwen, Daisy, Gabriel, Zoe, and Shiloh.

1 cup	packed brown sugar
½ cup	unsalted butter
2 lbs.	light corn syrup
12 slices	white or whole wheat bread
¼ cup	sugar
1 tsp.	cinnamon, divided
6	eggs, beaten
1½ cups	milk
1 tsp.	vanilla extract

Lightly grease a 9 x 13 baking dish and set aside. Bring brown sugar, butter, and corn syrup to a boil in a small saucepan. Remove from heat; pour into baking dish. Top with 6 slices bread; sprinkle with sugar and ½ teaspoon cinnamon. Top with remaining bread. Beat together eggs, milk, vanilla, and remaining cinnamon; pour over bread. Cover and refrigerate overnight. When ready to bake, remove dish from refrigerator. Preheat oven to 350°F. Bake uncovered 30–35 minutes. Makes 4–6 servings.

Berry-Apple Oatmeal "Pie"

2 cups	frozen berries, any kind
2 cups	rolled oats
½ cup	chopped nuts, any kind
1 tsp.	baking powder
½ tsp.	salt
1	red apple, peeled, cored, and grated
1 cup	milk
½ cup	vanilla yogurt
⅓ cup	maple syrup
2 tsp.	vanilla extract
2	eggs

Preheat oven to 375°F. Spray a 9-inch pie plate with nonstick cooking spray. In a bowl, stir together berries, oats, nuts, baking powder, salt, and apple. In another bowl, whisk together milk, yogurt, syrup, vanilla, and eggs. Add milk mixture to oat mixture. Stir well to combine. Spoon into pie plate and bake until firm, about 45–50 minutes. The top will be golden. Cut into slices and serve. Serves 6–8.

Chewy Granola Bars

6 cups	quick-cooking oats
⅓ cup	mixed dried fruit, coarsely chopped
1 cup	brown sugar, packed
1 cup	unsalted butter, melted
1 cup	light corn syrup
½ cup	miniature chocolate chips
½ cup	flaked coconut

Preheat oven to 350°F. In a large bowl, combine all ingredients. Spread into a greased jellyroll pan or 10 x 15 baking pan. Bake for 20 minutes or until edges are golden brown. Cool on a wire rack. Cut into bars or squares. Store in an airtight container or wrap bars individually. Makes about 3 dozen small bars.

Breakfast Parfaits

24 oz.	nonfat yogurt (any flavor)
4	fruit and cereal bars, cut into small cubes
6 oz.	fresh blueberries, blackberries, or raspberries
2 cups	fresh pineapple, finely chopped
¼ cup	wheat germ, flax seed, or chopped almonds, optional

Working in layers, spoon ingredients equally into 4 tall glasses and serve.

Eggs Gruyère

8 oz.	Gruyère cheese, shredded
4	eggs
2	bacon slices, cooked and crumbled
1 tsp.	chives, chopped
	freshly ground black pepper to taste
½ cup	bread crumbs

Preheat oven to 300°F. Spread half of the cheese in a greased 1-quart baking dish or pan. Break whole eggs onto cheese (don't mix the eggs), evenly spaced. Sprinkle bacon and chives over eggs; cover with remaining cheese. Season with pepper. Sprinkle bread crumbs over top. Bake for 15 minutes or until mixture is set. Slightly brown top under broiler. Serves 2–4

No-Crust Ham and Spinach Tart

2 tsp.	olive oil
1 cup	white onion, finely chopped
3	garlic cloves, minced
1 (10 oz.) pkg.	frozen chopped spinach, thawed and squeezed dry
4 slices	deli-style ham or turkey, sliced into strips
1 cup	milk
3	eggs
⅓ cup + 2 Tbs.	Parmesan cheese, grated
1 Tbs.	fresh basil, minced (or 2 tsp. dried basil)
½ tsp.	black pepper

Preheat oven to 350°F. Spray a 9-inch pie plate with nonstick cooking spray. Heat olive oil in a medium nonstick skillet over medium heat. Add onion and garlic and sauté for 2 minutes. Add spinach and ham. Stir well. Spread mixture into bottom of pie plate. Combine milk, eggs, ⅓ cup Parmesan cheese, basil, and pepper in a bowl. Pour over spinach mixture. Bake about 45–50 minutes, until knife inserted in center comes out clean. Sprinkle remaining Parmesan cheese over tart. Serve warm. Serves 6.

Tex-Mex Breakfast Casserole

1 lb.	mild ground pork sausage
1 sm.	white onion, chopped
½	green bell pepper, chopped
2 (10 oz.) cans	diced tomatoes and green chiles
8 (10 in.)	flour tortillas, torn into bite-size pieces
3 cups	Mexican blend cheese, shredded
6 lg.	eggs
2 cups	milk
1 tsp.	salt
½ tsp.	pepper

You can also cover and refrigerate casserole up to 8 hours before baking.

Preheat oven to 350°F. Spray a 9 x 13 casserole dish with nonstick cooking spray. Cook sausage in a large skillet over medium-high heat, stirring, until it crumbles and is no longer pink. Drain grease and return sausage to skillet. Add chopped onion and bell pepper and sauté over medium-high heat for 5 minutes or until vegetables are tender. Stir in tomatoes and green chiles; reduce heat and simmer 10 minutes. Layer half each of tortilla pieces, sausage mixture, and cheese in prepared baking dish. Repeat layers. Whisk together eggs, milk, salt, and pepper. Pour over layers in baking dish. Bake, lightly covered with aluminum foil, for 30 minutes or until golden and bubbly. Serves 6–8.

Sausage Pinwheels

2 cups	baking mix
½ cup	buttermilk (or milk)
1 lb.	breakfast sausage, mild or hot

If you're not going to bake immediately, wrap the roll in foil and freeze up to 1 month or refrigerate overnight.

Preheat oven to 400°F. Mix together baking mix and buttermilk and place on a lightly floured surface. Pat the dough into a 10 x 14 inch rectangle about ¼-inch thick. Crumble uncooked sausage evenly over the biscuit dough. Beginning at the long side, roll up jellyroll style into one long roll. Slice roll into ½-inch pinwheels. Place on baking sheet cut side up with the sides of each roll almost touching, and bake 15–18 minutes. Serve warm. Makes about 24 pinwheels.

Brown Sugar Bacon

1 lb.	bacon
1 cup	light brown sugar
1 Tbs.	cracked black pepper, optional

You don't have to twist the bacon, but it looks pretty.

Preheat oven to 425°F. Line a baking sheet with foil for much easier cleanup. Cut slices of bacon in half. Mix brown sugar and pepper in a bowl and sprinkle over each half-slice of bacon. Make sure you coat the slices well. Twist each slice and place on your baking sheet. Bake for 25 minutes until crisp. Serve at room temperature.

Slow Cooker Breakfast Potatoes

3 med.	baking potatoes, diced (peeling optional)
¾ cup	yellow onion, chopped
½ tsp.	seasoned salt (or regular salt)
4	bacon slices, cooked and crumbled
1 cup	cheddar cheese, shredded
1 Tbs.	water

Spray your slow cooker with nonstick cooking spray. Place half of the potatoes in the bottom. Sprinkle with half of the onions, half of the seasoned salt, half of the bacon, and half of the cheese. Repeat layers, then add water. Cover and cook on low heat for 6 hours or on high for about 3½ hours. Potatoes will be ready when they are fork-tender. Stir before serving. Serves 6.

Sweet Potato Breakfast Hash

½ lb.	bacon, cut into small pieces
2 sm.	onions, chopped
1	red bell pepper, cut into thin strips
	salt and pepper to taste
2 lbs.	sweet potatoes, peeled and cubed

Fry bacon in a skillet until cooked through, and drain on paper towel. In the same skillet, add onion, bell pepper, and a sprinkle of salt and pepper. Cook, stirring occasionally, until vegetables are softened. Add sweet potatoes and another sprinkle of salt. Cover and cook about 12 minutes, until potatoes are tender and starting to brown. Stir once or twice during that cooking time. Just before serving, add bacon and more salt or pepper, if desired. Serve warm. Makes 6–8 servings.

Breakfast Biscuit Sandwiches

Make these when you have leftover Restaurant-Style Biscuits!

6	eggs
½ tsp.	salt
½ tsp.	pepper
3 Tbs.	milk
¾ cup	chopped ham, cooked bacon, or cooked and crumbled sausage
½ cup	cheddar cheese, shredded
8	biscuits, warmed through

Whisk together eggs, salt, pepper, and milk in a bowl. In a skillet over medium heat, cook ham, bacon, or sausage for a couple of minutes until heated through. Turn down heat to medium-low and pour in egg mixture. Cook about 4–5 minutes, stirring constantly, until no longer runny. Add the cheese, stir again, and cook until cheese is melted. Slice open your biscuits and spoon eggs over bottom half of each. Cover with top halves of biscuits. Makes 8 big biscuits.

Breakfast Pizza

1 med.	potato, peeled and diced
4 tsp.	olive oil, divided
2 Tbs.	water
½ cup	bulk breakfast sausage
¼ cup	yellow onion, finely chopped
2	eggs, lightly beaten
2	whole wheat pitas
¼ cup	cheddar cheese, grated
¼ cup	salsa

In a small, covered pan, cook the diced potato in 2 teaspoons of olive oil and 2 tablespoons of water for 10 minutes, or until tender. While potato cooks, sauté sausage and onion in remaining 2 teaspoons of oil, breaking up with a fork or spoon, until sausage is cooked through. Add beaten eggs and gently scramble until fully cooked. Place half of egg mixture on top of each pita. Top with potatoes and cheese. Toast in a toaster oven or under the broiler until cheese is melted. Remove from oven and top with your favorite salsa.

Tex-Mex Egg Cups

8 (6 in.)	corn tortillas, warmed
1 (15 oz.) can	refried black beans
8	eggs
½ cup	salsa
¼ cup	Monterey Jack cheese, shredded

Preheat oven to 350°F and spray a regular 12-cup muffin tin with nonstick cooking spray (you'll be using only 8 of the 12 cups). Spray each warm tortilla with nonstick cooking spray on both sides, and press and fold each tortilla to fit into each muffin cup. Make 8 small balls of foil and place in each tortilla to help the "cups" hold their shape while baking. Bake 5 minutes. Remove foil and spread 2 tablespoons refried beans in the bottom of each tortilla cup. Make a little well in the center of the beans, and crack an egg into each well. Bake again until egg whites are set, about 15 minutes. Carefully remove tortilla cups from the muffin pan. Top each egg with a spoonful of salsa and sprinkle with cheese. Serve immediately. Makes 8.

Breakfast Mini-Quiches

1	prepared pie crust
8	eggs
⅔ cup	milk
1 cup	cheddar cheese, shredded
1 cup	ham, chopped, or bacon, crumbled and cooked

You can also add chopped onion or bell pepper to the filling.

Preheat oven to 375°F. Cut out 6 circles from the pie crust (about 3 inches in diameter) and place in greased muffin cups. Put muffin tin in refrigerator while you make the filling. In a bowl, beat together eggs, milk, cheese, and ham or bacon. Fill prepared muffin tins and bake 20–25 minutes or until puffy and slightly brown. Let cool 3 minutes and remove from tins. Serve warm or at room temperature. Makes 6.

Easiest Breakfast Casserole

1 loaf	French bread, torn into pieces
6	eggs
¼ cup	milk
¼ tsp. each	salt, pepper, and garlic powder
1 cup	mild or spicy Italian sausage, cooked and sliced
1 cup	Monterey Jack cheese, shredded

Preheat oven to 350°F. Spray a 9 x 13 baking pan with nonstick cooking spray. Distribute bread pieces in bottom of pan. Beat together eggs, milk, and seasonings; pour over bread. Sprinkle Italian sausage and cheese over casserole. Bake for 25 minutes or until top is golden brown and knife inserted in center comes out clean. Let rest 5 minutes before serving. Serves 10.

Breakfast Burritos

1 lb.	bulk breakfast sausage
1½ cups	frozen cubed hash brown potatoes
¼ cup	white onion, diced
¼ cup	green or red pepper, diced
4	eggs, beaten
12 (10 in.)	flour tortillas
½ cup	cheddar cheese, shredded
	salsa and sour cream, optional

In a large skillet, cook sausage over medium heat until no longer pink; drain. Add potatoes, onion, and pepper. Cook for 6 minutes, until tender, stirring once or twice. Add eggs, and stir while cooking until eggs are no longer runny. Spoon an even amount of egg filling in the center of each tortilla. Sprinkle with cheese. Fold ends over filling and roll up. Serve with salsa and sour cream, if desired. Makes 12 burritos.

Sunshine Smoothies

2	ripe bananas, peeled, sliced, and frozen
20	strawberries, stems removed and frozen
5 Tbs.	plain yogurt
2 cups	orange juice
¼ cup	honey

I keep banana slices in the freezer to make these smoothies anytime!

Combine all ingredients in a blender and process until thick and creamy. Serve immediately. Makes 4 small servings.

Vanilla Latte

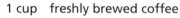

1 cup	freshly brewed coffee
½ cup	low fat milk
2 tsp.	vanilla extract

Just add sugar or sweetener as desired when you add the milk if you like your latte sweetened.

Pour coffee into 1 large coffee mug. Heat milk in small saucepan on low heat until warm, stirring briskly and constantly with a wire whisk to create foam. Remove from heat; stir in vanilla. Stir milk mixture into coffee.

Almond Milk Smoothie

1 cup	apple juice
1 cup	unsweetened almond milk
1 cup	fresh or frozen blueberries
1 cup	fresh or frozen strawberries
1 tsp.	vanilla extract
6	ice cubes (only if using fresh fruit)

Put all ingredients in a blender and purée until smooth. Pour into 4 glasses and serve.

CHAPTER 4

Sandwiches, Burgers, and Pizza

A smiling face is half the meal.

Latvian Proverb

I travel for work sometimes, and although I don't really like hotel rooms anymore, there has been one huge gift that has come from meeting the different kinds of people I find everywhere I go.

I've got good news. Most people I've met are kind, generous, and no different from you or me in that we all want a world that is safe and happy for those we love.

I spent a few intense days last year working with two people I had never met before. Jerry was a Jewish soup maker from Long Island, and Don was an Italian Catholic pasta maker from New Jersey. They saw me struggling with a heavy load of boxes, and although we hadn't even met yet, they both rushed over to help me. Over the next few days, they introduced me to important contacts I needed to meet, and they made sure I was safe in a big city I had never visited before.

By the end of the week, we knew all about each other's families, faiths, and shared love for good food. They had not met many South-erners before, and I could not help but smile when Don sincerely asked me if all Texans wore cowboy boots and if all Southern Baptists really did not drink or dance. They have become good friends.

On my flight home at the end of that week, we had just left the gate when suddenly we turned back, and someone hurriedly exited the plane.

The pilot announced that a crew member's wife had gone into labor, and we had returned to the terminal so he could hopefully make it to the hospital in time. We lost a lot of time because of this change of plans, but no one on board seemed to mind. Everyone clapped with the pilot's good news, and I heard more than one person share their labor and delivery stories.

We didn't need to know a single thing about this crew member or his wife. It didn't matter. We wanted the best for them, just like we want for ourselves and our children.

It seems that if we can get to know each other one-on-one—maybe over a hamburger or cup of coffee—many of the negative stereotypes we believe seem to disappear. It takes time and effort to invite someone you don't know well into your home for a meal, but I think it's one of the most loving acts of kindness we can offer one another.

After all, as Martin Luther King Jr. said, "We may have all come on different ships, but we're in the same boat now."

For health and strength and daily food,
we praise thy name O Lord.

Slow Cooker Pulled Pork Sliders

1 med.	yellow onion, chopped
½ cup	ketchup
⅓ cup	apple cider vinegar
¼ cup	brown sugar, packed
¼ cup	tomato paste
¼ cup	sweet paprika
¼ cup	Worcestershire sauce
¼ cup	prepared yellow mustard
1 Tbs.	salt
1 Tbs.	ground black pepper
1 (6 lb.)	boneless pork shoulder roast, cut into 4 pieces
25	soft rolls

In a 6-quart slow cooker, stir onion, ketchup, vinegar, brown sugar, tomato paste, paprika, Worcestershire, mustard, salt, and pepper until combined. Add pork to sauce mixture and turn to coat well with sauce. Cover slow cooker with lid and cook pork mixture on low heat for 8–10 hours, until pork is very tender. With tongs, transfer pork to large bowl. Turn setting on slow cooker to high; cover and heat sauce to boiling to thicken and reduce slightly. While sauce boils, shred the pork using two forks. Return shredded pork to slow cooker and toss with sauce to combine. Cover slow cooker and heat through if necessary. Serve on soft rolls.

Marinated Tuna Pita Pockets

8 oz.	mozzarella cheese, cubed
1 (6½ oz.) can	water-packed tuna, drained and flaked
1 cup	cherry tomatoes, quartered
½ sm.	red onion, sliced in thin rings
1 cup	celery, diced
¼ cup	olive oil
3 Tbs.	red wine vinegar
1 Tbs.	dried basil
½ tsp.	salt
¼ tsp.	black pepper
4	whole wheat pitas, warmed

Combine cheese, tuna, tomatoes, onion, and celery in a large bowl. In a smaller bowl, whisk together olive oil, red wine vinegar, basil, salt, and pepper. Pour over tuna mixture and stir gently to coat well. Cover and refrigerate at least 1 hour. To serve, cut pita pockets in half and spoon marinated tuna mixture into each pocket. Makes 8 pita halves.

Ultimate Ham and Cheese Sandwich

1 loaf	focaccia bread
3–4 Tbs.	olive tapenade
2	plum tomatoes, sliced
	olive oil, for drizzling
½ lb.	prosciutto or deli ham, thinly sliced
4	thin slices of mozzarella
4	fresh basil leaves
	black pepper to taste

Preheat oven to 375°F. Split focaccia in half horizontally to make 2 slices. On one half of the focaccia, spread olive tapenade and 4 slices of tomato. Drizzle other half with olive oil and top with sliced prosciutto or ham, mozzarella, and basil. Sprinkle with black pepper and close the sandwich. Bake for 3–4 minutes, just until cheese melts. Remove from oven and cut into 2–3 individual sandwiches. Serve warm.

Smoked Turkey Wraps

2 lg.	sweet yellow onions, diced
1 Tbs.	sugar
2 Tbs.	vegetable oil
2 tsp.	balsamic vinegar
2 (6½ oz.) pkgs.	garlic and herb cheese spread, softened
8 (10 in.)	flour tortillas
1½ lbs.	thinly sliced smoked turkey
1 lb.	bacon slices, cooked and crumbled
3 cups	mixed baby salad greens

To caramelize onions, heat vegetable oil in a skillet over medium-high heat; add onions and sugar and cook about 15 minutes, stirring frequently. Onions will turn a caramel color when ready. Stir in vinegar and set aside. Spread cheese evenly over tortillas. Top with caramelized onions, turkey, bacon, and mixed greens. Roll up and wrap in foil or waxed paper. Refrigerate until ready to eat, up to 4 hours. Best when cut in half before serving. Makes 8.

Miniature Reuben Sandwiches

½ cup	Thousand Island dressing
1 (16 oz.) loaf	miniature (party-size) rye bread, sliced
6 oz.	Swiss cheese slices, halved
12 oz.	corned beef, thinly sliced
1 (16 oz.) can	shredded sauerkraut, well-drained

Make sandwiches ahead of time and freeze in resealable plastic bags. When ready to bake, follow directions for baking sheets and increase cooking time to 15–20 minutes.

Preheat oven to 375°F. Spray 2 baking sheets with nonstick butter-flavored cooking spray. Spread dressing on one side of each slice of bread. Top half of the bread slices with a half-slice of cheese, corned beef, sauerkraut, and then remaining half-slice of cheese. Top with remaining slices of bread. Place sandwiches on one baking sheet. Place the second baking sheet, coated side down, on top of the sandwiches. Bake for 10 minutes, until cheese is melted. Makes about 20 sandwiches.

My Favorite Fish Sandwich

¼ cup	mayonnaise
1–1½ tsp.	wasabi paste
2 Tbs.	rice vinegar
2 cups	cabbage, thinly sliced
	salt and pepper to taste
4 (5 oz.)	white fish fillets, such as grouper or mahi-mahi
½ cup	panko (Japanese style bread crumbs)
3 Tbs.	vegetable oil
4	sandwich buns, split, buttered, and toasted
4	lemon wedges

Mix mayonnaise with wasabi paste and rice vinegar. Toss with cabbage. Season with salt and pepper. Place slaw in refrigerator. Sprinkle fish with salt and pepper. Place panko in a shallow dish. Dredge fish in panko, turning over to completely cover both sides. Heat oil in a nonstick skillet to medium-high heat. Add fish and sauté until fish is opaque in the center, about 4–5 minutes on each side. Panko will be golden brown. Top the bottom half of each bun with a fish fillet. Squeeze lemon juice over. Spoon slaw over fish, and top with other half of bun. Serve immediately.

Meatball Super Heroes

1 lb.	sweet Italian sausages, casings removed
3 cups	marinara sauce, divided
½ cup	Parmesan cheese, freshly grated
⅓ cup	fresh basil, chopped and divided
4 (6 in.)	hoagie-style sandwich buns
1 cup	mozzarella cheese, shredded

Combine sausages, ½ cup marinara sauce, Parmesan, and 2 tablespoons of the basil. Shape into 8 meatballs (2 per sandwich). Add meatballs to a large skillet, along with remaining marinara and basil. Bring to a boil. Cover and reduce heat to a simmer. Cook, turning the meatballs often, about 20 minutes or until no longer pink inside. When you are ready to make the sandwiches, preheat oven to 400°F. Place the bottom half of each hoagie on a baking sheet. Spread 2 tablespoons of meatball sauce over each bun. Cut meatballs in half, and place four halves on each bun, cut sides down. Spoon remaining sauce over, and top with mozzarella. Bake for only about 5 minutes, until cheese is melted. Cover with tops of hoagies and serve immediately.

Best BLTs

1 cup	mayonnaise
2 cups	fresh basil
	salt and pepper
12 slices	rustic white bread
3 lg.	ripe tomatoes, sliced
1 lb.	thick-sliced bacon, cooked to a crisp
2	ripe avocadoes, peeled, pitted, and sliced
1	red onion, thinly sliced
6	butter lettuce leaves (or any other lettuce)

For the ultimate sandwich, add a fried egg over tomatoes.

Mix mayonnaise and basil in a food processor until mixture is blended and basil is chopped. Add salt and pepper to taste. Process 3 more seconds. Store in refrigerator until ready to use. When ready to make sandwiches, top 6 slices of bread with mayonnaise mixture and tomato slices. Sprinkle with salt and pepper, if desired. Layer bacon, avocado, onion, and lettuce over tomatoes. Spread mayonnaise over other 6 slices of bread and place facedown on top of each sandwich. Cut and serve immediately. Serves 6.

Grilled Apple Cheddar Sandwich

4 slices	whole grain bread
2 tsp.	Dijon mustard or mayonnaise
1	red apple, cored and very thinly sliced
½ cup	sharp cheddar cheese, shredded
2 Tbs.	unsalted butter, softened

Spread 1 slice of bread with half of mustard or mayonnaise and arrange half of apple slices on top. Add ¼ cup cheese and top with second slice of bread. Repeat for second sandwich. Spread butter on the outside of all bread slices. Heat a skillet over medium heat. Add sandwiches and cook, turning once, until golden brown and cheese is melted. Transfer to a plate and serve immediately. Serves 2.

Peanut Butter and Banana Paninis

2 Tbs.	unsalted butter
3	bananas, sliced into ¼-inch slices
¾ cup	light brown sugar
dash	cinnamon
1–1½ cups	peanut butter
8 slices	whole wheat bread
1 Tbs.	unsalted butter, melted

Heat a large nonstick skillet over medium-high heat. When hot, add 1 tablespoon of butter, then add bananas. Brown bananas for 30 seconds without stirring. Turn bananas over, then add brown sugar, cinnamon, and remaining butter. Cook about 1 minute more, stirring gently, until sugar is melted and bananas are caramelized but still solid. Remove from heat. Heat another skillet over medium-high heat, or if you have a panini press, heat it to 375°F. Spread peanut butter on 1 side of 4 slices of bread. Top with a single layer of caramelized bananas. Top sandwiches with remaining bread slices. Brush melted butter on the outside of the sandwiches, and grill 2–3 minutes on each side until bread is toasted. Serve immediately. Serves 4.

Chicken Parmesan Sandwiches

2	egg whites, lightly beaten
½ cup	Italian-seasoned bread crumbs
¼ cup	Parmesan cheese, grated
8	boneless, skinless chicken breast tenders
1 Tbs.	olive oil
1 cup	marinara sauce, warmed
½ cup	mozzarella cheese, shredded
4	sandwich buns, sliced in half

Preheat oven broiler. Place egg whites in a shallow dish. Mix bread crumbs and Parmesan cheese in another dish. Dip chicken first in egg whites, then bread crumb mixture. Coat well. Heat olive oil in a large nonstick skillet over medium-high heat. Add chicken tenders. Cook 3 minutes per side, until no longer pink inside. Remove from heat and keep warm. Spread 1 tablespoon of marinara sauce over bottom half of each bun. Top with 2 chicken tenders per bun, cutting chicken if needed to fit. Top with additional sauce and mozzarella cheese. Arrange on baking sheet. Place under broiler until cheese is melted. Remove and top with other half of buns. Serve warm.

Chicken Broccoli Pockets

1½ cups	cooked chicken breast, chopped
2 cups	broccoli florets, diced, steamed until just tender
¾ cup	cheddar cheese, shredded
⅓ cup	Swiss cheese, shredded
	salt and pepper to taste
4 (8 in.)	flour tortillas

Preheat oven to 400°F. Spray a baking sheet with nonstick cooking spray. Combine chicken, broccoli, and cheeses in a bowl. Season with salt and pepper, and stir to combine. Place a packed ½ cup of chicken mixture in center of each tortilla. Fold about a ½ inch of right and left sides in, then tightly roll up tortilla from top to bottom.

Place tortilla pockets seam-side down on baking sheet. Bake until crisp and beginning to turn golden, about 12 minutes. Cut in half at a diagonal, and serve immediately.

Rosemary Chicken Salad Sandwiches

3 cups	cooked chicken breast, chopped
½ cup	green onions, chopped
⅓ cup	roasted almonds, chopped
¼ cup	plain yogurt or sour cream
¼ cup	mayonnaise
2 tsp.	fresh rosemary, chopped
1 tsp.	Dijon mustard
	salt and pepper to taste
10 slices	whole grain bread, toasted

This chicken salad is also wonderful stuffed in ripe, red tomatoes.

Combine all ingredients except bread. Spread about ¾ cup of chicken mixture over each of 5 toast slices. Top with remaining toast slices. Makes 5 sandwiches.

Smoked Turkey Pepper Jelly Paninis

8 slices	your favorite bread
¼ cup	red or green jalapeño pepper jelly
12 oz.	sliced smoked deli turkey
4 med.	Gruyère cheese slices
3 Tbs.	unsalted butter, melted

Spread pepper jelly over 1 side of 4 slices of bread. Top each with turkey, Gruyère cheese, and second slice of bread. Heat a nonstick skillet over medium-high heat. Brush 1 side of each sandwich with melted butter and place facedown in skillet. Brush remaining side with rest of butter. Grill sandwiches 3–4 minutes per side, until golden brown and cheese has started to melt. Serve warm. Makes 4.

Super Hero Sandwiches

½ cup	vinaigrette dressing
4	submarine-style rolls, split in half horizontally
1 cup	roasted red bell peppers, cut into strips
8 oz.	thinly sliced ham
8 oz.	thinly sliced salami
8 oz.	thinly sliced provolone cheese
2 sm.	tomatoes, sliced
1 head	iceberg lettuce, shredded
½ med.	red onion, thinly sliced, if desired

Drizzle the bottom half of each roll with vinaigrette dressing. Layer peppers, ham, salami, cheese, tomato slices, lettuce, and onion on top. Replace tops of rolls, pressing down firmly. Cut in half and serve cold. Makes 4.

BBQ Chicken Sliders

2 lbs.	lean ground chicken or turkey
¼ cup	water
	salt and pepper
2 Tbs.	vegetable oil
1 lg.	sweet onion, chopped
½ cup	barbecue sauce
16	potato rolls, split in half
1 cup	smoked Gouda cheese, grated, optional

Place the chicken or turkey and water in a bowl. Season with salt and pepper, and mix well. Form ground chicken or turkey into 16 slider-size patties to fit rolls. Spray a nonstick skillet with cooking spray and cook burgers over medium heat, about 4–5 minutes per side. Remove patties from skillet and keep warm. Heat oil in same skillet. Add onions and cook over medium heat until softened and caramel in color. Add barbecue sauce to onions and heat through. Place each burger on bottom half of rolls. Spoon a bit of the onion mixture over, and 1 tablespoon of cheese per slider, if desired. Cover with tops of rolls and serve. Makes 16 sliders.

Smoky Beef Burgers

½ cup	mayonnaise
2 Tbs.	chipotle pepper in adobo sauce, minced, divided
1½ lbs.	ground beef chuck
2 tsp.	smoked paprika
1 tsp.	salt
1 lg.	red onion, sliced
1 Tbs.	olive oil
4	hamburger buns, grilled or toasted
8	bacon slices, cooked until crispy
	Monterey Jack cheese, lettuce, tomatoes, or avocado to garnish, as desired

Combine mayonnaise and 1 tablespoon chipotle pepper. Set aside. Using your hands, mix ground beef with remaining tablespoon chipotle pepper, smoked paprika, and salt. Form into 4 patties. Refrigerate until ready to use. In a skillet over medium heat, sauté red onion in olive oil until onions are softened and caramel in color, about 15 minutes. Set aside. Heat gas or charcoal grill to medium. Grill beef patties until they reach 160°F on an instant-read thermometer, approximately 5–6 minutes on each side.

To assemble, spread chipotle mayonnaise on each hamburger bun. Top with burger patty, caramelized onions, and bacon slices. Garnish burgers as desired.

Open-Face Portobello Mushroom Burgers

¼ cup	mayonnaise
½ cup	roasted red peppers (from a jar), chopped
2	garlic cloves, minced
	salt and pepper to taste
4 lg.	portobello mushrooms, stems removed
4 slices	red onion, about ½-inch thick
4 slices	sourdough bread, at least ½-inch thick
3 Tbs.	olive oil
4 slices	Swiss cheese, optional

Combine mayonnaise with red peppers and garlic. Season with salt and pepper, if desired. Brush mushrooms, onions, and bread slices with olive oil. Grill over medium heat until vegetables are tender and bread is light brown. Bread will be ready in about 5 minutes; vegetables will need 10–12 minutes. To serve, spread red pepper mayonnaise over 1 side of each slice of bread. Top with mushroom, onion slice, and cheese, if desired. Serve with a green salad on the side.

Vegetarian Spicy Black Bean Burgers

4 cups	canned black beans, drained and rinsed
½ cup	panko (Japanese style bread crumbs)
2 lg.	eggs
4	green onions, minced
3 Tbs.	fresh cilantro, chopped
2	garlic cloves, minced
2 tsp.	ground cumin
1½ tsp.	dried oregano
2 tsp.	crushed red pepper flakes
1 tsp.	coarse salt
½ tsp.	ground black pepper

Place 2 cups of black beans in a food processor or blender and pulse until chunky. Transfer to a large mixing bowl. Add remaining whole black beans plus panko, eggs, green onion, cilantro, garlic, cumin, oregano, and red pepper flakes, and mix until well combined. Shape into 4–6 patties, depending on how big you like your burgers. Place patties on a plate in the refrigerator for 15 minutes.

When ready to cook, remove patties from refrigerator. Sprinkle with salt and pepper. Heat an ungreased skillet until very hot. Add burgers to skillet. Cook for about 4 minutes on first side, until seared. Flip and cook second side for 5 minutes, turning down the heat to medium. Best served immediately on a bun with cheese, avocado, and salsa. Makes 4–6 burgers.

MOPS Mom: Stuffed Pesto Turkey Burgers

■ *Alicia Odell, Fulshear, Texas* ■

Alicia grew up with a mom who was a fantastic cook. In fact, she was so good, Alicia preferred to let her do all the cooking! But after Alicia married her husband, Jeremy, she began to learn how to cook, calling on her mom for lessons. "For a long time I would make only the main dish," Alicia said. "Eventually Jeremy asked if we could have a side with our meal!" Now that Alicia and Jeremy have a son, she tries to make sure each meal is balanced. "We have another child on the way, and I am determined to cook healthy for our family so we can live long and enjoy our life together!"

8 oz.	prepared pesto
1 lb.	ground turkey
2 sticks	mozzarella string cheese, cut in half crosswise
1 Tbs.	olive oil

In a large bowl, combine pesto and ground turkey and mix well. Form mixture into 4 patties, leaving a small amount in the bowl. Push 1 piece of cheese into the middle of each patty. Use the remaining ground turkey to cover the top of the cheese. Heat oil in pan to medium heat, and cook patties until they are no longer pink, about 8 minutes per side. These can be eaten alone or on a bun with your choice of condiments.

Teriyaki Burgers

1½ lbs.	ground beef
½ lb.	ground pork
½ cup	teriyaki sauce
2 Tbs.	minced garlic
⅔ tsp.	black pepper
¼–½ cup	Italian-seasoned bread crumbs
¼ cup	ice water
8 slices	provolone cheese
8	hamburger buns, toasted

Combine ground beef and pork with teriyaki sauce, minced garlic, pepper, and bread crumbs. Cover and refrigerate overnight, up to 24 hours. Just before making into patties, add the ice water and mix well. Shape into 8 quarter-pound patties. Make an indention in the center of each burger with your thumb. This helps keep burgers flat. Grill or broil until no longer pink and internal temperature reaches 160°F. Top with provolone cheese. Serve on hamburger buns with desired toppings. Makes 8.

Pimento Cheeseburgers

1 cup	sharp cheddar cheese, grated
3 Tbs.	mayonnaise
1 tsp.	lemon juice
1 Tbs.	pimentos, diced
1 Tbs.	onion, minced
1	garlic clove, minced
½ tsp.	hot pepper sauce
	salt and black pepper
1½ lbs.	ground beef, divided into 4 equal patties
1 Tbs.	canola oil
4	hamburger buns, warmed
	lettuce, tomato, cooked bacon to garnish, if desired

You can always use purchased pimento cheese if you're in a hurry, but I do think homemade usually tastes better.

Mix together cheese, mayonnaise, lemon juice, pimentos, onion, garlic, hot pepper sauce, and a pinch of salt and pepper. Set aside. Season each beef patty with salt and pepper. Heat a large skillet over medium-high heat. Add canola oil and patties. Cook burgers for 12–14 minutes, flipping halfway through, until no longer pink. Turn off heat. Spread 1 tablespoon of pimento cheese spread over each burger. Cover skillet and let sit 2 minutes, until pimento cheese begins to melt. Serve immediately on prepared hamburger buns with desired garnishes. Makes 4.

Grilled Tofu Burgers

½ cup	soy sauce
2 Tbs.	sugar
1 Tbs.	apple cider or rice vinegar
14 oz.	extra firm tofu, well-drained and sliced into 4 (1 in.) patties
2 Tbs.	canola oil
¼ lb.	Monterey Jack cheese, sliced
4	whole wheat hamburger buns, toasted
	honey mustard, pickles, sunflower seeds, and alfalfa sprouts to garnish, if desired

In a saucepan, combine soy sauce, sugar, and vinegar. Cook over low heat until thickened, 5–7 minutes. Place tofu patties in a bowl and pour the marinade over. Let sit 20 minutes, turning once. Heat oil in a nonstick skillet or griddle over medium heat. Cook tofu 2 minutes per side, watching carefully. Top each patty with cheese slices and cook until cheese melts, about 2 minutes. Serve on toasted hamburger buns with desired condiments and toppings. Makes 4.

Brisket Burgers

2 lbs.	beef brisket, ground (ask your butcher)
	salt and pepper to taste
6 slices	smoked cheddar cheese, or any cheese of your choice
6	hamburger buns, split and toasted
	pickle slices, coleslaw, and red onion slices to garnish, if desired

Note: these burgers are worth the effort of asking your butcher to help you.

Place ground meat in a large bowl and season with salt and pepper. Give it about 3 turns in the bowl with your hands or a big spoon and it's done. Shape into 6 patties. Heat a large nonstick skillet over medium heat. Spray with nonstick cooking spray. Cook burgers 7 minutes per side for medium, adding cheese during the final minute or so to melt. Remove burgers to a plate. Serve on buns with desired condiments. Serves 6.

Greek Lamb Burgers with Yogurt Sauce

For the sauce:

2 cups	plain Greek yogurt
½ cup	feta cheese, crumbled
½ cup	white onion, chopped
½	cucumber, peeled, seeded, and diced
1 Tbs.	garlic, minced
2 tsp.	fresh lemon juice
	salt and pepper

For the burgers:

1 lb.	ground lamb
⅔ cup	bread crumbs
½ cup	white onion, chopped
2 Tbs.	fresh parsley, chopped
3 tsp.	garlic, minced
1 tsp.	dried oregano
½ tsp.	salt
1 tsp.	black pepper
4 (6½ in.)	pita bread rounds
4	lettuce leaves

For the sauce, mix all ingredients together in a bowl. Season with salt and pepper to taste. Store in refrigerator until ready to use. For the burgers, mix lamb, bread crumbs, onion, parsley, garlic, and oregano in a large bowl. Blend well. Season with salt and pepper. Shape mixture into 4 equal ¾-inch patties. Preheat oven broiler. Place lamb patties on broiler pan or baking sheet lined with foil. Broil 4 minutes per side, until no longer pink. Heat pita round in microwave for about 30 seconds. Open pitas and place one lettuce leaf and burger inside each pita. Top with a large spoonful of yogurt sauce. Serve immediately, with additional sauce as needed. Makes 4.

MOPS Favorite: Turkey Club Deluxe Pizza

1 (13.8 oz.) can	refrigerated pizza crust or your favorite crust for a 12-inch round
2 tsp.	sesame seeds
6	bacon slices
¼ cup	reduced-calorie mayonnaise
1 tsp.	lemon juice
1 cup	Monterey Jack cheese, shredded
1 tsp.	dried basil
4 oz.	deli turkey breast slices, cut into 1-inch strips
1 sm.	tomato, diced
½ cup	Swiss cheese, shredded

Preheat oven to 425°F. Prepare crust; sprinkle with sesame seeds. Bake 10–12 minutes. While crust is baking, cook and crumble bacon. Combine mayonnaise and lemon juice in small bowl. Spread mayonnaise mixture over slightly cooled crust. Top with Monterey Jack cheese, basil, turkey, bacon, and tomatoes. Sprinkle with Swiss cheese. Bake 7–9 minutes or until crust is light brown and cheese is melted. Serves 4–6.

Easy Pesto Pizza

1 (12 in.)	prebaked pizza crust
3 Tbs.	pesto
3	plum tomatoes, sliced
4 oz.	fresh Mozzarella cheese, thinly sliced
⅓ cup	pitted ripe olives, sliced
1 Tbs.	fresh oregano, minced

Preheat oven to 450°F. Place the pizza crust on a cookie sheet. Spread pesto evenly over crust. Top with tomato slices, mozzarella cheese, and olives. Bake for 8 minutes or until cheese is melted. Sprinkle with oregano. Makes 4 servings.

Black Bean and Chicken Pizza

1 (12 in.)	prebaked pizza crust
1 Tbs.	olive oil
½	garlic clove, minced
6 oz.	frozen grilled chicken breast strips, thawed
1 cup	Alfredo sauce
6 oz.	mozzarella cheese, shredded
½ cup	canned black beans, drained
4 oz.	canned, sliced jalapeño peppers, optional

Preheat oven to 450°F. Heat olive oil in a skillet over medium-low heat. Add garlic and stir just until fragrant. Add chicken strips and cook until heated through. Spread Alfredo sauce over crust, and sprinkle on a third of the shredded cheese. Arrange chicken strips over cheese, and sprinkle with black beans. Top with jalapeños if desired. Cover with remaining cheese. Place pizza directly on oven rack. Bake for 15 minutes, until cheese is melted and bubbly.

Sun-Dried Tomato Shrimp Pizza

1 (12 in.)	prebaked pizza crust
½ cup	sun-dried tomato pesto
2 cups	cooked medium shrimp, peeled and deveined
1 (6 oz.) jar	artichoke hearts, drained
½ cup	fontina cheese, shredded

Preheat oven to 450°F. Spread pesto over pizza crust. Arrange shrimp and artichoke hearts over pesto. Sprinkle with cheese. Bake for 8–10 minutes, until cheese is melted and lightly browned at the edges.

White Four-Cheese Pizza

3 Tbs.	olive oil
1	garlic clove, minced
1 (13.8 oz.) can	refrigerated pizza dough
6 oz.	mozzarella cheese, shredded
3 oz.	soft goat or feta cheese, crumbled
½ cup	part-skim ricotta cheese
3 Tbs.	Parmesan cheese, freshly grated
3 Tbs.	fresh basil, thinly sliced

This is a great appetizer too.

Preheat oven to 450°F. Brush a 9 x 13 metal baking pan with 1 tablespoon olive oil. Mix remaining 2 tablespoons oil with garlic in small bowl. Roll out pizza dough on lightly floured work surface to 10 x 14 inch rectangle. Transfer dough to prepared pan, pinching the dough edges in the pan to make the outer crust. Brush lightly with some of the garlic oil. Top with mozzarella cheese and goat cheese, leaving a ½-inch border. Crumble ricotta cheese over. Sprinkle with Parmesan. Bake until crust is golden brown and cheese melts, about 18 minutes. Drizzle remaining garlic oil over pizza. Let stand 3 minutes. Cut pizza into desired number of pieces. Sprinkle with basil. Transfer to platter and serve hot. Makes up to 32 small squares.

Cheese Steak Pizza

1 (12 in.)	prebaked pizza crust
½ cup	pizza sauce
1½ cups (16 oz.)	sliced deli roast beef, cut into strips
½	green or red bell pepper, seeded and cut into strips
½ cup	onion, chopped
1 cup	cheddar cheese, shredded
1 cup	mozzarella cheese, shredded

Preheat oven to 425°F. Spread pizza sauce on crust. Arrange beef, bell pepper, and onions over sauce. Sprinkle cheddar and mozzarella evenly over pizza. Bake about 15 minutes or until cheeses are melted and bubbly and crust is crisp and golden.

Naan and Goat Cheese Pizza

1 (4 ct.) pkg.	naan (Indian flatbread)
	olive oil
4 oz.	soft goat cheese
1 (10 oz.) jar	roasted red pepper and artichoke tapenade
½ cup	fresh cilantro, chopped

Any kind of prepared tapenade will taste great on this pizza.

Preheat oven to 400°F. Place naan on cookie sheets, brush with olive oil, and warm in the oven for about 5–10 minutes. Remove from oven and spread a thin layer of goat cheese on each naan. Spread a light layer of tapenade over goat cheese. Sprinkle with cilantro and place back in oven for 5–10 more minutes, until goat cheese is softened.

Deep-Dish Pepperoni Pizza

2 (28 oz.) cans	diced tomatoes, well-drained
3	garlic cloves, minced
2 tsp.	dried oregano
2 tsp.	dried basil
1 Tbs.	cornmeal
1 (1 lb.) loaf	frozen bread dough, thawed
4 cups	mozzarella cheese, shredded
8 oz.	pepperoni, sliced
⅓ cup	Parmesan cheese, grated
1 tsp.	olive oil

For a smooth sauce, simply purée tomatoes in blender or food processor.

Preheat oven to 425°F. Combine tomatoes, garlic, oregano, and basil in a bowl. Spray a deep-dish 12-inch pie pan (or pizza pan if you have one) with nonstick cooking spray. Sprinkle cornmeal over bottom. On a lightly floured surface, roll bread dough into a 13-inch circle, as evenly as possible. Place dough in pie pan, making sure dough reaches all the way up the sides. Spread half of tomato sauce over. Sprinkle with half of the mozzarella cheese and half of the pepperoni. Repeat sauce, cheese, and pepperoni layers. Top with Parmesan. Drizzle pizza with olive oil. Bake 35–40 minutes, until cheese is bubbly and crust is browned.

97

Mexican Pizza

2 cups	cooked chicken, shredded
1 tsp.	taco seasoning mix
1 cup	salsa, divided
1 Tbs.	water
1 (12 in.)	prebaked pizza crust
2 cups	cheddar or Mexican blend cheese, shredded
¼ cup	black olives, sliced
¼ cup	green onion, chopped
½ cup	canned black beans, drained and rinsed
1	avocado, diced
1	tomato, diced

Preheat oven to 450°F. Combine chicken with taco seasoning mix, ½ cup salsa, and water. Spread remaining ½ cup salsa over pizza crust. Top with chicken mixture and cheese. Then sprinkle olives, green onions, and black beans over cheese. Bake 8–10 minutes until cheese is melted. Remove from oven and cool slightly. Top with avocado and tomato. Serve immediately.

Buffalo Chicken Pizza

¾ cup	crushed tomatoes
¼ cup	honey
1	garlic clove, minced
½ tsp.	dried oregano
½ tsp.	hot pepper sauce, or to taste
1 cup	cooked chicken breast, diced
1 (13.8 oz.) can	refrigerated pizza dough
1 Tbs.	olive oil
¾ cup	blue cheese, finely crumbled

If your family doesn't eat blue cheese, use mozzarella cheese instead. Just increase the amount to 1½ cups and sprinkle over chicken before baking.

Preheat oven to 500°F. In a saucepan, combine tomatoes with honey, garlic, oregano, and hot pepper sauce. Simmer over low heat for 5 minutes. Mix ¼ cup tomato mixture with chicken and set aside. Unroll pizza dough onto large, lightly greased baking sheet, building up edges slightly. Brush with olive oil. Spread remaining tomato sauce over dough. Sprinkle chicken mixture over sauce. Bake until lightly browned, about 10 minutes. Remove from oven. Sprinkle with blue cheese. Cut pizza into 6 wedges.

Greek Hummus Pizza

1 (13.8 oz.) can	refrigerated pizza dough
7 oz.	hummus, any flavor
½ cup	tomatoes, chopped
½ cup	red bell pepper, chopped
3 slices	red onion, separated into rings
⅓ cup	pitted black olives, sliced
1½ cups	mozzarella cheese, shredded

Preheat oven to 450°F. Roll pizza crust dough into a large oval, and place on greased baking sheet. Spread hummus over crust; top with remaining ingredients. Bake pizza for 10–12 minutes or until cheese is melted and crust is browned.

Italian Sausage and Tomato Pizza

2 tsp.	vegetable oil
1 lb.	frozen pizza dough, thawed, or 1 (13.8 oz.) can refrigerated pizza dough
¾ cup	marinara sauce
1 cup	provolone cheese, shredded
1 cup	grape or cherry tomatoes, halved
½ med.	red onion, thinly sliced
¼ lb.	Italian sausage, cooked and crumbled
	salt and pepper to taste

Preheat oven to 450°F. Brush a large baking sheet with oil. On a lightly floured work surface, roll and stretch dough into a 10 x 15 inch rectangle. Transfer to prepared sheet. Spread marinara sauce over dough, leaving a 1-inch border around edges. Top with provolone, tomatoes, and onion. Sprinkle sausage over top and season with salt and pepper. Bake until crust is golden and cheese is melted, about 20 minutes. Serve immediately.

MOPS Mom: Chicken Wing Pizza

Julie Jones, Camp Lejeune, North Carolina

1 (13.8 oz.) can	refrigerated pizza dough
¼ cup	unsalted butter, melted
¼ cup	hot chicken wing sauce
2½ cups	cooked chicken breast, chopped
½ cup	ranch dressing
2 cups	cheddar cheese, shredded
2 Tbs.	fresh cilantro, chopped

Preheat oven to 450°F. Brush a large baking sheet with oil. On a lightly floured work surface, roll and stretch dough into a rectangle. Transfer to prepared sheet. Spread ranch dressing on pizza crust. Melt butter and mix with hot chicken wing sauce. Mix butter mixture with chopped chicken, and spread evenly over pizza. Sprinkle with cheese. Bake 10–12 minutes until cheese is melted. Sprinkle with cilantro and serve.

Barbecue Chicken Pizza

1 lb.	frozen grilled chicken breasts, thawed and cut into bite-size pieces
1 cup	barbecue sauce
1 lb.	frozen pizza dough, thawed, or 1 (13.8 oz.) can refrigerated pizza dough
2 cups	mozzarella cheese, shredded
¼ cup	red onion, slivered, optional

Preheat oven to 400°F. Combine chicken and barbecue sauce. Brush a large baking sheet with oil. On a lightly floured work surface, roll and stretch dough into a rectangle. Transfer to prepared sheet. Spread chicken and barbecue sauce over dough. Top with cheese. Sprinkle with onion, if desired. Bake 20–25 minutes until cheese is melted and bubbly.

Vegetarian Flatbread Pizza

1 (18 x 12 in.)	lavash flatbread
4 Tbs.	olive oil, divided
½ cup	kalamata olives, sliced or chopped
1 cup	Monterey Jack cheese, shredded
2 cups	feta cheese, crumbled
1½ cups	mushrooms, sliced
½ cup	red onion, chopped
¾ cup	marinated artichoke hearts, chopped
1 cup	tomatoes, chopped
	salt to taste

Preheat oven broiler. Place flatbread on large baking sheet. Brush with 2 tablespoons of olive oil. Broil 1 minute. Change oven to bake at 450°F. Turn flatbread over and brush with remaining oil. Sprinkle with olives, cheeses, mushrooms, onion, artichoke hearts, and tomatoes. Sprinkle with salt. Bake about 10 minutes. Cut into squares and serve hot.

CHAPTER 5

Table Talk

The family dinner table is a great place for meaningful conversation, but sometimes I need help to get family talk to go beyond "yes" or "no" answers. Here are a few questions and ideas to keep family conversation flowing.

Tell us one thing that happened today that made you feel silly (or happy, loved, smart, etc.).

Tell us one thing that really happened to you today, and make up another thing that did not really happen. Let us guess which one is true.

Do you have a hero? Mine is . . . because . . .

One thing I want to learn to do that I can't do now is . . .

What is the very first thing you can remember about your life?

If you could have picked your own name, what would it be? Why?

God made each of us with our own special gifts and talents. What do you think is one of your gifts or talents? Let each family member also share about the other family members' talents.

People always talk about being "successful." What do you want to do in your life to feel like you are a success?

Would you rather be a professional athlete, president of your country, or a movie star? Why?

Do you have a best friend? What do you like about him or her?

If you could pick your own allowance each week, how much would you want? What would you do with it?

Have you ever felt peer pressure to do something you didn't want to do? How did you handle it?

What do you think is your best physical feature?

Would you rather be great at one thing or okay at a lot of things?

Do you have an all-time favorite toy?

Do you think you have ever been punished unfairly?

What is the most enjoyable thing our family has done together?

If you could pick two things our family could do together this weekend, what would you pick?

What would you do if you were invisible for a day?

What was the best part of your day? What was the worst?

What's your worst nightmare? Favorite dream?

Name one thing you are afraid of. I am afraid of . . .

What's your most embarrassing moment?

If you could have a free day to do anything you wanted, what would you choose to do?

What are three things you want to do before you die?

If you could compete in the Olympics, what sport would you choose?

If you could choose our next family vacation, where would we go?

You get to choose our family's next dinner. What are we having?

If you get invited to a friend's house, but then you get another invitation to a party you really want to attend, what should you do?

Tell us the last joke you remember hearing.

Has a movie ever made you cry? What happened?

Who is someone you would like to help?

Where is one place in the world you never want to go?

Where is one place in the world you really want to visit?

If you could tell me to never cook a certain food again, what would it be?

If you knew a friend of yours had stolen something, what would you do about it?

If you could trade lives with somebody you know, who would it be?

You're stuck on a deserted island. What three things do you wish you had with you?

Let's each think of three things we are grateful for in our lives.

If you could invent something that would make life easier, what would it do?

My favorite Bible verse is . . . because . . . What's yours? Let's memorize each other's favorite verses.

Does our family seem too busy? What should we change?

What is something that makes you nervous?

Teach us one thing you learned today that you don't think we yet know.

What is the grossest thing you have ever eaten?

Finish this sentence. "I have never . . ."

Let's make a story together. I'll start with the first sentence, and then you make up the next sentence.

If you could read someone's mind, would you? What would you do with the information?

What movie character would you want to be?

If you could ask God one question, what would it be?

CHAPTER 6

Soups and Salads

Worries go down better with soup.

Jewish Proverb

There is one thing I find difficult to do if I am angry with someone: eat with them. It's as if I have completely forgotten how to chew and swallow when I have to share a table with someone who has hurt me in some way. Every bite seems like torture.

But what's worse is not doing it. Presbyterian minister and author Frederick Buechner said it best when he said that anger may be the most fun of all the deadly sins.

> To lick your wounds, to smack your lips over grievances long past, to roll over your tongue the prospect of bitter confrontations still to come, to savour to the last toothsome morsel both the pain you are given and the pain you are giving back—in many ways it is a feast fit for a king. The chief drawback is that what you are wolfing down is yourself. The skeleton at the feast is you.[1]

It takes tremendous humility to put away forever whatever disagreement you have had with your spouse, child, or friend, and offer them a way back into your life.

1. Frederick Buechner, *Wishful Thinking: A Theological ABC* (New York: HarperCollins, 1973), 2.

Food Family Style

Churches split, countries divide, families fight, and neighbors build fences. But food has a way of bringing us together, no matter how different we may think we are. We all have to eat, three times a day if we're fortunate. And as simple as it sounds, the table has a way of putting us all on a level playing field. Over hearty soup and warm, buttered bread, we look across the table and remember that we're not so different after all.

For food that stays our hunger,
for rest that brings us ease,
for homes where memories linger,
we give our thanks for these.

Bistro Tomato Basil Soup

4 cups	crushed tomatoes
4 cups	low-sodium tomato juice
14	fresh basil leaves, plus additional for garnish
1 cup	whipping cream
½ cup	unsalted butter, softened
¼ tsp.	cracked black pepper
	salt to taste

This recipe doubles easily, but it is best to work in batches.

Combine tomatoes and tomato juice in a saucepan. Simmer for 30 minutes over medium-low heat. Cool slightly. Add basil, and in small batches, purée in a blender or food processor. Return mixture to saucepan. Add cream and butter. Stir over low heat until butter and cream are incorporated. Stir in pepper and salt to taste before serving. Garnish with fresh basil leaves. Serve with hot, crusty French bread.

MOPS Mom: Potato Soup

■ *Sarah Clark, Raleigh, North Carolina* ■

1 lg.	yellow onion, chopped
2 Tbs.	vegetable oil
4 lbs.	potatoes, peeled and diced
2 (14.5 oz.) cans	chicken broth
1 lb.	cooked ham, diced
2 (12 oz.) cans	evaporated milk
4 cups	sharp cheddar cheese, grated

Brown onions in oil in a large stockpot or Dutch oven. Add potatoes and broth. Cook on medium-low heat until potatoes are fork tender. Add ham and evaporated milk. Bring to a simmer. Add cheese. Cook on low heat until cheese is melted and soup is heated through.

Slow Cooker French Onion Soup

5 sm.	yellow onions, thinly sliced
2 (10 oz.) cans	beef consommé (in soup aisle)
2 (14 oz.) cans	beef broth
1 pkg.	dry onion soup mix
8 sm. slices	French bread, toasted
1 cup	Gruyère, Swiss, or provolone cheese, shredded

Combine onions, consommé, broth, and soup mix in slow cooker. Cook on high for 4 hours or low for 8 hours. To serve, ladle soup into oven-safe bowls. Place 1 slice of toasted French bread over soup in each bowl. Sprinkle cheese over, and melt under oven broiler. Serves 8.

Creamy White Bean and Spinach Soup

3 Tbs.	olive oil
3 cups	yellow onion, chopped
3	garlic cloves, minced
1 Tbs.	fresh rosemary, chopped
5 cups	chicken broth
2 (15 oz.) cans	white beans, drained
1 (15 oz.) can	chickpeas, drained
1 (6 oz.) bag	baby spinach
	salt and pepper to taste
	Parmesan cheese, grated

Heat oil in a large pot over medium-high heat. Add onions and garlic. Sauté until softened, about 12 minutes. Add rosemary and stir for 1 minute. Add broth, white beans, and chickpeas. Bring to a low boil. Reduce heat and simmer 10 minutes. Working in small batches, place soup in a blender and purée until smooth. Return purée to soup pot. Add spinach and cook just until wilted, about 1 minute. Add salt and pepper to taste. Top each bowl with Parmesan cheese. Makes 4 regular or 8 small servings.

Summer Vegetable Soup

2 Tbs.	olive oil
2 cups	yellow onion, chopped
2	zucchini, diced
2	yellow summer squash, diced
2 (15 oz.) cans	white beans, undrained
2 (14 oz.) cans	chicken broth
8 oz.	cooked ham, diced
1	red, ripe tomato, seeded and diced
2 Tbs.	pesto

Heat oil in a medium saucepan over medium heat. Add onion and cook until softened, about 6 minutes. Add zucchini and squash and cook 5 minutes, stirring occasionally. Lower heat to a simmer and stir in undrained beans, broth, ham, and tomato. Stir in pesto. Heat through and serve with additional pesto, if desired.

Roasted Red Pepper Soup

2 cups	roasted red bell peppers, peeled and seeded
2 (32 oz.) cans	stewed tomatoes, drained
3 Tbs.	olive oil
2	garlic cloves, minced
3 cups	chicken broth
	salt and pepper to taste

Purée peppers and tomatoes together in a food processor. Heat olive oil in a large pot on low heat. Add garlic and sauté gently for 2 minutes. Add purée and chicken broth. Bring to a boil. Season with salt and pepper to taste. Delicious hot or cold.

Sarah's Cheese Vegetable Soup

Sarah is a friend of mine who always makes wonderful soup! She shared this recipe in our church cookbook years ago, and I make it each fall as soon as the weather turns cool.

Use Mexican cheese loaf and/or cooked, diced chicken for variety.

4 cups	frozen cubed hash browns
1 cup	yellow onion, chopped
1 (16 oz.) pkg.	frozen mixed vegetables
6 cups	chicken broth
2 (10 oz.) cans	condensed cream of chicken soup
1½ lbs.	processed cheese loaf, cubed

In a large stockpot, combine hash browns, onion, mixed vegetables, and chicken broth. Bring to a boil, then simmer 15 minutes. Add cream of chicken soup and mix well. Add cheese cubes to soup. Stir until cheese is melted. Makes 6–8 servings.

Healing Chicken Noodle Soup

2 Tbs.	olive oil
¾ cup	celery, diced
1–1¼ cups	carrots, diced
½ tsp.	salt
½ tsp.	black pepper
2 qts.	chicken stock
2½ cups	wide egg noodles
3 cups	cooked chicken, shredded
1 tsp.	fresh thyme

You can also add 1 cup diced yellow onion with the celery and carrots.

Heat oil in a large stockpot or Dutch oven over medium heat. Add celery, carrots, salt, and pepper. Stir and cook until vegetables are softened, about 10 minutes. Slowly pour in chicken stock. Bring to a boil, and add egg noodles. Stir once, and allow noodles to cook 10 minutes (do not overcook). Add chicken and thyme and heat through. Serve hot.

Lighter Tortilla Soup

8	corn tortillas, halved and thinly sliced
1 Tbs.	canola oil
3	poblano peppers, seeded and diced
1 med.	white onion, diced
1 tsp.	ground cumin
1 lb.	boneless, skinless chicken breasts, cut into 1-inch pieces
4 cups	reduced-sodium chicken broth
1 (10 oz.) can	diced tomatoes with green chiles, undrained
2 Tbs.	fresh lime juice
	salt and pepper to taste
½ cup	reduced fat sharp cheddar cheese, shredded
¼ cup	fresh cilantro, chopped

Add diced avocado and a dollop of reduced fat sour cream to garnish.

Preheat oven to 400°F. Spray a baking sheet with nonstick cooking spray, and place tortilla strips on the sheet in a single layer. Bake until crisp, about 12–13 minutes. Set aside. While tortillas are baking, heat oil in a large saucepan over medium-high heat. Add peppers and onions. Cook, stirring constantly, until vegetables are softened, about 4 minutes. Add cumin and cook 1 minute. Add chicken, broth, and undrained tomatoes. Bring to a boil, and reduce heat and simmer until chicken is no longer pink, about 15 minutes. Remove from heat. Stir in lime juice. Add salt and pepper to taste. To serve, top each bowl of soup with baked tortilla strips, cheese, and cilantro. Serves 6.

Chicken and Wild Rice Cream Soup

6 Tbs.	unsalted butter
¼ cup	all-purpose flour
2 cups	half-and-half
3 cups	chicken broth, divided
1½ cups	cooked wild rice
1 cup	cooked chicken, chopped (I use rotisserie chicken)
½ cup	yellow onion, chopped
½ cup	celery, sliced
	salt and pepper to taste

Heat the butter in a large saucepan over medium heat. Add the flour and whisk until blended. Cook for 2 minutes, stirring constantly; do not allow to brown. Add the half-and-half and 1 cup of the broth gradually, whisking constantly until blended. Bring to a boil and cook for several minutes, stirring frequently.

Add the remaining 2 cups broth, wild rice, chicken, onion, and celery and mix well. Season to taste with salt and pepper and simmer for 30 minutes, stirring occasionally. Serves 8.

Southwestern Chicken Soup

1 (12 oz.) jar	salsa verde (green salsa)
3 cups	cooked, shredded chicken breast
1 (15 oz.) can	cannellini beans or black beans, drained
3 cups	chicken broth
1 tsp.	ground cumin, optional
2	green onions, chopped
½ cup	sour cream
	tortilla chips

Cook salsa in a large saucepan over medium-high heat for 2 minutes, then add chicken, beans, broth, and cumin. Bring to a boil, lower heat to a simmer, and cook for 10 more minutes, stirring occasionally. Top each bowl of soup with a sprinkling of onions, a spoonful of sour cream, and some tortilla chips.

White Chicken Chili

1 Tbs.	olive oil
2	yellow onions, chopped
4	garlic cloves, minced
2 (4 oz.) cans	chopped green chiles
2 tsp.	ground cumin
1½ tsp.	dried oregano
¼ tsp.	ground cloves
¼ tsp.	cayenne pepper
3 (15 oz.) cans	great northern beans, drained
1 (14 oz.) can	chicken broth
1	rotisserie-style chicken, skinned and shredded, or 1½ lbs. cooked, chopped chicken breast
3 cups	Monterey Jack cheese, shredded
	salt and pepper to taste
	sour cream, salsa, chopped cilantro, or chopped jalapeño pepper to garnish

Heat olive oil in large saucepan over medium-high heat. Sauté onions in hot oil for 10 minutes or until tender. Stir in garlic, green chiles, cumin, oregano, cloves, and cayenne pepper. Sauté for 2 minutes. Add beans and broth and bring to a boil. Reduce heat and simmer 45 minutes, stirring occasionally. You may prepare to this point up to 1 day in advance and store, covered, in refrigerator. Bring to simmer before continuing recipe. Add chicken and 1 cup of cheese to bean mixture and mix well. Simmer until cheese melts, stirring frequently. Season to taste with salt and pepper. Ladle into bowls and garnish as desired with remaining cheese, sour cream, salsa, cilantro, or jalapeño pepper. Serves 8.

Slow Cooker Chicken Fajita Soup

1 Tbs.	olive oil
1 cup	onion, diced
½ cup	green onions, chopped
1	red or green bell pepper, seeded and diced
1	jalapeño pepper, seeded and diced
2 lbs.	ready-to-serve chicken fajita meat, cut into bite-size pieces
1 pkg.	taco seasoning mix
4 cups	vegetable juice (such as V-8)
1½ cups	black bean and corn salsa
	cheddar or Monterey Jack cheese, sour cream, and tortilla chips to garnish

You can change the intensity of the heat by adding more or less jalapeño pepper.

In a skillet over medium heat, sauté onions, green onions, bell pepper, and jalapeño pepper in olive oil for three minutes, until softened. Place in slow cooker and add chicken, seasoning mix, vegetable juice, and salsa. Cook on low for 6 hours. Ladle into 4 serving bowls and top each with grated cheese, sour cream, and tortilla chips as desired. Serve with warm flour tortillas.

Slow Cooker Black Bean Chili

2 lbs.	ground chuck
2 cups	onion, chopped
2	garlic cloves, chopped
2 Tbs.	chili powder
1 tsp.	ground cumin
1 tsp.	paprika
1 tsp.	oregano
1 tsp.	salt
½ tsp.	cayenne pepper
2 cups	beef stock (use less for thicker chili)
2 (10 oz.) cans	diced tomatoes with green chiles
3 (15 oz.) cans	black beans, drained and rinsed

In a medium skillet, brown the ground chuck over medium heat. Once browned, drain the fat from the meat and return to skillet. Add onion and garlic and continue to cook and stir over medium heat until onion is transparent.

Transfer meat mixture to a slow cooker or stockpot. Add all remaining ingredients. Stir to combine. Cook in slow cooker on low for 5–7 hours, or simmer in a stockpot for 45 minutes, covered, plus an additional 30 minutes uncovered, stirring occasionally. Serve with your favorite toppings (such as cheese, onions, or jalapeños) and corn bread.

MOPS Favorite: Italian Tortellini Soup

1 lb.	bulk sweet Italian sausage
1 cup	yellow onion, chopped
2	garlic cloves, crushed
5 cups	beef stock
1 (16 oz.) can	chopped tomatoes
1 (8 oz.) can	tomato sauce
2 Tbs.	dried basil
2 Tbs.	dried oregano
1 lg.	carrot, peeled and sliced
1 (10–12 oz.) bag	frozen or refrigerated cheese-filled tortellini
1 lg.	zucchini, peeled and sliced
	Parmesan cheese for sprinkling

In a stockpot or Dutch oven, brown sausage with onion and garlic. Drain. Add beef stock, tomatoes, tomato sauce, and spices; bring to a low boil. Add carrots and simmer 10–15 minutes. Add tortellini and zucchini; continue cooking until zucchini is tender, about 15–20 minutes. Ladle into soup bowls and top with a sprinkle of Parmesan cheese. Serves 8–10.

MOPS Favorite: Magic Beef Stew

1 lb.	stew beef
3	celery stalks, sliced
1	yellow onion, coarsely chopped
3	carrots, peeled and sliced
3 lg.	potatoes, peeled and cubed
2 tsp.	salt
½ tsp.	black pepper
1 Tbs.	sugar
2 Tbs.	quick-cooking tapioca
1½ cups	tomato juice

Preheat oven to 275°F. Place beef evenly in a heavy, deep pan or Dutch oven. Arrange vegetables over top. Combine salt, pepper, sugar, and tapioca, and sprinkle over vegetables. Pour tomato juice over. Cover pan tightly with foil or lid. Bake 4 hours. Do not peek or stir, and a delicious, hearty stew will "magically" appear, thanks to the thickening of the tapioca. Serves 6.

Slow Cooker Sausage and Bean Soup

1 lb.	bulk sweet Italian sausage or turkey sausage, browned and crumbled
1 (16 oz.) can	corn, drained
1 (16 oz.) can	pinto beans, drained
1 (16 oz.) can	kidney beans, drained
1 (16 oz.) can	black beans, drained
1 (16 oz.) can	great northern beans, drained
1 (16 oz.) can	diced potatoes, drained
1 (10 oz.) can	Mexican-style tomatoes with green chiles
1 (14 oz.) can	beef broth
1 pkg.	beef stew seasoning
2 cups	water

Mix all ingredients together in slow cooker. Cook on low 8–10 hours.

Lamb and Barley Stew

2 Tbs.	unsalted butter
2	carrots, chopped
2 lg.	celery stalks, chopped
1	yellow onion, chopped
2	garlic cloves, minced
1 cup	pearl barley, rinsed
4 cups	beef broth
3 cups	cooked lamb, cut into ½-inch pieces

Cooked beef or chicken can be used as well.

Melt butter in a heavy stockpot over medium heat. Add carrots, celery, onion, and garlic. Sauté about 8 minutes, until vegetables start to soften. Add barley and cook 2 minutes, stirring. Add broth. Simmer until barley is tender, about 45 minutes. Add lamb and heat through.

Clam Chowder

2 oz.	bacon, chopped
1	sweet yellow onion, chopped
1 cup	celery, chopped
2	garlic cloves, minced
½ Tbs.	all-purpose flour
2 cups	bottled clam broth
2 med.	baking potatoes, peeled and cubed
1 tsp.	Old Bay seasoning
1 cup	heavy cream
2 cups	fresh clams (or 14 oz. canned clams), minced

You can use regular or fat free half-and-half instead of heavy cream, but your chowder won't be quite as thick.

Fry bacon in a large stockpot or Dutch oven over medium-high heat, until crispy. Remove bacon and let drain on paper towel. Add onion, celery, and garlic to stockpot. Cook and stir for 1 minute. Add flour and cook 2 more minutes, stirring constantly. Stir in clam broth. Then add potatoes, seasoning, and cream. Stir and cook at a low simmer for 15 minutes. Add clams. Cook and stir for 2 minutes.

Thai Coconut Soup

½ Tbs.	vegetable oil
1 Tbs.	fresh ginger, grated
½ stalk	lemongrass, minced
1 tsp.	red curry paste
2 cups	chicken broth
1½ Tbs.	fish sauce
½ Tbs.	light brown sugar
2 (6¾ oz.) cans	unsweetened coconut milk
¼ lb.	fresh shiitake mushrooms, sliced
½ lb.	medium shrimp, peeled and deveined
1 cup	steamed white rice
1 Tbs.	fresh lime juice
	salt to taste
2 Tbs.	fresh cilantro, chopped

Heat oil in a large pot over medium heat. Stir in ginger, lemongrass, and curry paste and cook for 1 minute. Slowly pour in chicken broth, stirring continually. Stir in fish sauce and brown sugar. Simmer for 15 minutes. Stir in coconut milk and mushrooms and cook until mushrooms are softened, about 5 minutes. Add shrimp; cook until no longer translucent, about 5 minutes. Stir in rice and lime juice. Season with salt; garnish with cilantro. Serve hot.

MOPS Favorite: Seven Layer Salad

2 cups	lettuce, chopped
1 cup	cauliflower, chopped
1 cup	celery, chopped
1 cup	green onions, chopped
1 (10 oz.) pkg.	frozen green peas, thawed
1 cup	tomatoes, chopped
1 cup	mayonnaise
8 oz.	Swiss or cheddar cheese, shredded
½ lb.	bacon slices, cooked and crumbled

Layer vegetables in a large bowl. Spread mayonnaise over top. Sprinkle with grated cheese and crumbled bacon. Cover salad and refrigerate. Will keep in refrigerator for several days. Serves 8.

Potluck Marinated Vegetable Salad

½ cup	vegetable oil
¾ cup	apple cider vinegar
½ cup	sugar
1 tsp.	salt
1 tsp.	pepper
1 (15 oz.) can	shoe peg corn, drained
1 (16 oz.) can	English peas, drained
1 (17 oz.) can	French style green beans, drained
1 (15 oz.) can	hominy, drained
1 (2 oz.) jar	chopped pimentos, drained
1 cup	chopped celery
1	red pepper, chopped
1	green pepper, chopped
1 bunch	green onions, chopped

Combine first five ingredients in a medium saucepan. Bring to a boil, stirring, until sugar is dissolved. Cool. Combine vegetables in large bowl; add vinegar mixture and toss to coat. Cover and refrigerate for 12 hours, stirring occasionally. Serves 8.

MOPS Mom: Shrimp and Mango Pasta Salad

■ *Jennifer Beach, Williamsburg, Virginia* ■

Jennifer Beach found a recipe for shrimp and mango pasta salad in a magazine, and as an experienced cook, she played with the recipe to make it her own. "I worked at Williams-Sonoma for a few years and learned lots," Jennifer said. Jennifer and her husband, Russ, have one daughter. "She is our miracle baby, as we struggled with infertility for over eight years," she shared. "So, being a mommy is my favorite job ever. I love MOPS because it allows me some time with other women and allows my daughter Rebecca a chance to make friends. It is nice to know that the day-to-day things I deal with are normal."

1	avocado, peeled and diced
1 Tbs.	fresh lime juice
1 Tbs.	fresh lemon juice
1 lb.	small shrimp, cooked, peeled, and deveined
1 lb.	any shape pasta, cooked, drained, and rinsed
1	mango, peeled and diced
½ cup	frozen kernel corn, thawed
½ med.	red onion, finely diced
1 Tbs.	mango juice (squeeze the pit over the bowl)
2 tsp.	olive oil
2 Tbs.	fresh cilantro, optional
	salt and pepper to taste

Toss avocado in a large mixing bowl with lemon and lime juices. Add remaining ingredients and toss to combine. Chill and serve.

Pasta Club Salad

1 cup	mayonnaise
2 Tbs.	white wine vinegar
2 Tbs.	fresh lemon juice
12 oz.	rotini pasta, cooked and drained
4	chicken breasts, cooked and cubed
5	bacon slices, cooked crisp and crumbled
1 cup	cherry tomatoes, quartered
½ cup	Swiss cheese, cut into thin strips
	salt and pepper to taste

Blend mayonnaise, vinegar, and lemon juice. Combine with pasta, chicken, and bacon. Refrigerate at least 1 hour. Before serving, toss with tomatoes and cheese. Add salt and pepper to taste. Serves 6.

BLT Salad

¼ cup	olive oil
¼ cup	Parmesan cheese, grated
2 Tbs.	mayonnaise
1 Tbs.	lemon juice or vinegar
⅛ tsp	salt
¼ tsp.	black pepper
6 cups	romaine lettuce, torn into pieces
1 cup	cherry or grape tomatoes, halved
3	green onions, sliced
4	bacon slices, cooked crisp and crumbled

For a thinner dressing, add 1 tablespoon of water to dressing and whisk.

For the dressing, whisk together oil, Parmesan cheese, mayonnaise, lemon juice or vinegar, salt, and pepper. In your salad bowl, combine lettuce, tomatoes, onions, and bacon. Toss with dressing.

Turkey Apple Salad

2 Tbs.	plain Greek yogurt or sour cream
2 Tbs.	mayonnaise
1 Tbs.	white vinegar
¼ tsp.	salt
¼ tsp.	black pepper
1 cup	leftover roasted turkey or chicken, shredded
½ cup	celery, sliced
1	granny smith apple, cut into bite-size pieces
3 Tbs.	toasted walnuts, chopped
1 sm. head	green or red leaf lettuce

In a large bowl, whisk together yogurt or sour cream, mayonnaise, vinegar, salt, and pepper. Toss with turkey, celery, apple, and walnuts. When ready to serve, place 3 lettuce leaves on each plate and top with turkey apple salad.

Ginger Salmon Salad

⅔ cup	lime juice
½ cup	honey
1 Tbs.	soy sauce
½ tsp.	fresh ginger, minced
4 (6 oz.)	salmon fillets, skin removed
¼ tsp.	salt
4 cups	spring mix salad greens
1 cup	mango, peeled and sliced

Preheat oven broiler. In a small bowl, combine lime juice, honey, soy sauce, and ginger. Set aside ½ cup for later. Place salmon on a foil-lined baking sheet coated with cooking spray. Baste salmon fillets with ½ cup lime juice mixture. Broil 4–6 inches from heat for 4–5 minutes on each side, basting occasionally with more lime juice mixture. Remove from oven and sprinkle with salt. Divide salad greens among 4 plates; top with salmon and mango slices. Drizzle with reserved ½ cup lime juice mixture.

Fresh Summer Corn Salad

4	ears corn, shucked (or 3 cups frozen corn, thawed)
1½ Tbs.	olive oil
3	red, ripe tomatoes, diced
1	cucumber, peeled, seeded, and chopped
¼ cup	red onion, minced
1	green or red bell pepper, seeded and chopped
3 Tbs.	fresh cilantro, chopped
	salt and pepper to taste
2 Tbs.	apple cider vinegar

Preheat oven to 400°F. Place foil on bottom of baking sheet. Remove corn from cob and place in a small bowl. Combine with olive oil. Spread on baking sheet. Roast corn in oven 7–8 minutes, stirring once. Set aside. When cooled, toss corn with remaining ingredients. Refrigerate 2 hours before serving. Serve alongside your favorite grilled meat.

Crunchy Asian Slaw

1 sm. head	Napa cabbage, shredded
2 lg.	carrots, peeled and grated
1	red bell pepper, seeded and thinly sliced
1 tsp.	canola oil
2 tsp.	sesame oil
1 Tbs.	rice or white vinegar
2 tsp.	soy sauce
	juice of 1 lime
½ tsp.	sugar
¼ tsp.	red pepper flakes, optional
2 Tbs.	dry roasted peanuts, chopped, or sunflower seeds

Combine cabbage, carrots, and bell pepper in a large bowl. In a small bowl, combine canola oil, sesame oil, rice or white vinegar, soy sauce, lime juice, sugar, and red pepper flakes. Drizzle over vegetables and toss well. Refrigerate until serving, up to 3 hours. Add peanuts or sunflower seeds just before serving.

125

Strawberry Spinach Salad

1 (10 oz.) pkg.	baby spinach leaves
1 cup	fresh strawberries, hulled and quartered
¼ cup	feta cheese
¼ cup	Parmesan cheese, grated
1 cup	dried cranberries
1 cup	slivered almonds
3 Tbs.	raspberry vinaigrette salad dressing

Just before serving, toss spinach with all remaining ingredients in a large bowl. Serves 4–6.

Easy Greek Salad

5 med.	red, ripe tomatoes
2 med.	cucumbers, peeled, seeded, and cut into chunks
1 sm.	red onion, sliced thinly and separated into rings
8 oz.	feta cheese, crumbled
18	kalamata olives
5 Tbs.	olive oil
3 Tbs.	red wine or balsamic vinegar
1 tsp.	dried oregano
1 tsp.	salt
½ tsp.	black pepper
1 head	romaine lettuce, rinsed, dried, and torn into pieces

Cut each tomato into 8 wedges. Toss with cucumbers, onion, feta, and olives. Combine olive oil, vinegar, oregano, salt, and pepper, and shake well. Place romaine in a large salad bowl and top with tomato mixture. Drizzle dressing over, and toss well to combine. Serves 6.

Buttermilk Coleslaw

½ cup	buttermilk
2 Tbs.	mayonnaise
1 sm.	shallot, minced
½ tsp.	cider vinegar
½ tsp.	sugar
¼ tsp.	Dijon mustard
⅛ tsp.	black pepper
1 lb.	cabbage, shredded
1 med.	carrot, peeled and shredded

Try adding chopped green onion and/or diced, seeded jalapeños to this recipe.

Mix buttermilk, mayonnaise, shallot, vinegar, sugar, mustard, and pepper in a small bowl. Combine cabbage and carrot in a large bowl. Pour dressing over and toss to coat. Refrigerate until chilled, about an hour.

Curried Rice Salad

2 Tbs.	olive oil, divided
1 Tbs.	curry powder
1 cup	long-grain brown rice
2½ cups	water
¼ tsp.	salt
½ tsp.	black pepper
¼ cup	fresh lime juice
1 cup	red seedless grapes, halved, or raisins
½ cup	fresh mint, chopped
½ cup	roasted cashews, chopped

Use quick-cooking brown rice to reduce cooking time. Follow package directions.

Heat 1 tablespoon oil in a medium saucepan over medium-high heat. Add curry powder and cook for 30 seconds, stirring constantly. Add rice, water, salt, and pepper. Stir. Bring to a boil, and then reduce heat to low. Cover and cook until rice is tender, about 1 hour. Remove from heat and let stand 10 minutes. Transfer to a bowl and stir in lime juice. Cover and refrigerate about 1 hour. Just before serving, stir in grapes, mint, and cashews. Serves 6.

Italian Caprese Salad

3 Tbs.	fresh lemon juice
½ tsp.	salt
½ tsp.	black pepper
3 Tbs.	olive oil
1¼ lbs.	tomatoes of any kind (red, yellow, cherry, grape, etc.)
6 oz.	fresh mozzarella cheese, sliced
6	fresh basil leaves, thinly sliced

Whisk together lemon juice, salt, and pepper. Gradually add olive oil. Set aside. Cut all large tomatoes in ⅓-inch slices. Cut cherry-type tomatoes in half. Arrange all tomatoes and cheese on your salad platter. Drizzle dressing over. Sprinkle with basil.

Honey Berry Salad

2 med.	firm bananas, peeled and sliced
2 cups	fresh blueberries
2 cups	fresh blackberries or raspberries
2 cups	sliced fresh strawberries
⅓ cup	honey
1 tsp.	lime juice
½ tsp.	poppy seeds
2 Tbs.	fresh mint, chopped, optional

In your serving bowl, combine all of the fruit. In a small bowl, combine honey, lime juice, and poppy seeds. Pour over fruit and toss to coat. Add mint and toss again, if desired.

Winter Pear Salad

5 Tbs.	olive oil
2 Tbs.	balsamic vinegar
1 tsp.	honey
1 tsp.	Dijon mustard
1 Tbs.	green onion, finely chopped
	salt and pepper
4 cups	mixed greens
2	ripe pears, cored and thinly sliced
2 oz.	Asiago cheese, shaved with vegetable peeler
½ cup	unsalted or lightly salted cashews, toasted

In a lidded jar, combine olive oil, balsamic vinegar, honey, mustard, green onion, and salt and pepper to taste. Cover, shake well, and set aside. In large bowl, combine greens and ⅔ of the dressing. Divide salad onto plates, and arrange pear slices over in spiral pattern. Drizzle with additional dressing. Top with shaved Asiago cheese and toasted cashews. You can also simply toss all ingredients in a large salad bowl.

Pesto Pasta Salad

1 cup	mayonnaise
3 Tbs.	pesto
½ tsp.	garlic salt
¼ cup	vinegar
½ tsp.	black pepper
6 cups	cooked pasta, such as rotini or penne
3	green onions, chopped
1½ cups	cherry tomatoes, halved or quartered
3 Tbs.	pine nuts, toasted
⅔ cup	Parmesan cheese, grated

Try cubed fresh mozzarella in place of the Parmesan cheese

For the dressing, combine mayonnaise, pesto, garlic salt, vinegar, and pepper. Combine remaining ingredients and toss with dressing. Serve chilled or at room temperature. Serves 6.

Broccoli Ramen Salad

1 cup	walnut pieces
1 pkg.	ramen noodles, broken into pieces (discard seasoning packet)
¼ cup	unsalted butter
1 cup	vegetable oil
½ cup	sugar
½ cup	rice vinegar
3 Tbs.	soy sauce
	salt and black pepper to taste
3 sm. heads	romaine lettuce, washed and torn
2 cups	raw broccoli florets, washed and chopped
4	green onions, chopped

Sauté walnuts and ramen noodles in melted butter until golden brown. Set aside to drain on paper towel. To make dressing, in a lidded jar combine vegetable oil, sugar, rice vinegar, soy sauce, and salt and pepper to taste. Cover tightly and shake well. When ready to serve, toss romaine, broccoli, and green onions together in a large salad bowl. Top with walnut and ramen mixture, and drizzle dressing over. Toss again. Serves 8.

Berry Salad with Vanilla-Yogurt Dressing

4 cups	fresh berries, such as strawberries, blueberries, and raspberries
1 cup	low fat vanilla yogurt
¼ cup	honey
¼ tsp.	vanilla extract
1½ Tbs.	skim milk, if needed
	cinnamon to taste
	fresh mint leaves, optional

Wash, stem, and sort berries. In a small bowl combine yogurt, honey, and vanilla and whisk together. Add cinnamon to taste and stir until well incorporated. Add milk until you reach your desired consistency, which should be thin enough to drizzle over fruit. Place berries in serving bowls and drizzle with yogurt dressing. Garnish with mint, if desired, and serve immediately. Serves 8.

German Potato Salad

2 lbs.	yellow potatoes, unpeeled
½ lb.	bacon, cooked until crisp and crumbled (reserve 1 Tbs. drippings)
1 lg.	white onion, chopped
2 Tbs.	canola oil
3 Tbs.	coarse ground mustard
6 Tbs.	apple cider vinegar
1 cup	green onions, chopped
½ tsp.	salt
½ tsp.	black pepper

Boil potatoes in a large pot until tender, about 15 minutes, but do not let them cook until they fall apart when stabbed with a fork. Drain and cool slightly. Peel, if desired, and cut into bite-size chunks.

In a skillet over medium heat, add onion to reserved bacon fat and cook until softened and light brown, about 7 minutes. Remove from heat. Prepare dressing by combining oil, mustard, vinegar, green onions, salt, and pepper. Toss dressing with bacon, potatoes, and white onion. Serve warm or at room temperature.

Italian Salad

6 cups	romaine lettuce, torn into bite-size pieces
1 cup	red bell pepper, cut into strips
1 cup	yellow bell pepper, cut into strips
½ cup	red onion, thinly sliced
½ cup	pitted black olives
½ cup	mozzarella cheese, shredded
¼ cup	pepperoncini, stem ends trimmed, seeded, and sliced
1–1½ cups	Italian dressing or vinaigrette

In a large bowl, combine lettuce, peppers, onion, olives, mozzarella cheese, and pepperoncini, and toss well with vinaigrette. Serve chilled. Serves 6.

Thai Noodle Salad

15 oz.	dried soba or whole wheat noodles, broken into pieces
2 tsp.	sesame oil
⅓ cup	rice vinegar
⅓ cup	soy sauce
2 Tbs.	fresh lime juice
2 Tbs.	light brown sugar
3	garlic cloves, minced
1 cup	carrots, finely grated
¼ cup	salted peanuts, coarsely chopped
½ cup	fresh cilantro, chopped

In a large pot, cook noodles according to package directions. Drain and rinse noodles. Set aside. In a large bowl, whisk together sesame oil, rice vinegar, soy sauce, and lime juice. Add brown sugar and garlic. Whisk until sugar is dissolved. Toss in noodles, carrots, peanuts, and cilantro.

Cover and refrigerate at least 1 hour. Toss again before serving. Serves 6–8.

CHAPTER 7

Main Dishes

A recipe has no soul. You, as the cook, must bring soul to the recipe.

Thomas Keller

In the grocery store the other day, I overheard a woman saying that she plans her family meals a month at a time, and it has revolutionized her life. One day of cooking gets her thirty days of meals in the freezer.

I couldn't help but imagine what this woman could accomplish in Washington, DC, under budget and on time. She has my vote hands down.

I looked at my cart containing one lonely head of lettuce and a package of chicken breasts, and wished for the millionth time that I could sit down on a Saturday afternoon and plan the week's meals. Believe me, I've tried. I design menu spreadsheets, knowing my life would be much simpler if I could make a pot roast on Monday, shred it for tacos on Tuesday, and use it for stroganoff on Wednesday. But for some reason, I tend to rebel against the idea that I have to decide on Monday what I might be hungry for on Friday.

Occasionally I daydream of living in a place in which the course of the day includes walking to the local market to visit with the farmers, talk to the fishermen, and purchase the food needed only for that day. We eat what's fresh for that moment and never dream of stockpiling cases of sports drinks. We find the beauty of an elegant sufficiency.

Food Family Style

One night, my family was running way behind schedule, everyone was starving, and I was trying to get chicken on the table for supper. Our younger son begged to be allowed to use the kitchen mallet to help flatten the chicken breasts. It was not going to get dinner on the table most efficiently, but I gave in to his enthusiasm. The usual boring task became one of the funniest things I've ever seen. His older brother recorded this slapping-chicken routine on video, and our family has laughed about it for months. Efficient? No. Was dinner an hour later than normal? Yes. But great joy is hidden in these ordinary moments. We just have to open our eyes and hearts to the times where the means is mysteriously the end, and life itself is a picture of God's good grace.

Father, you are the giver of all good gifts. And we thank you for the gift of laughter. Slow us down, Lord, and open our eyes and ears to hear the laughter inside each of us. For it is your Spirit within us that we desire to please. Amen.

Chipotle Chicken Tostadas

4 (8 in.)	corn tortillas, or purchased whole tostadas
1 cup	barbecue sauce
1 Tbs.	canned chipotle pepper in adobo sauce, chopped
2 cups	cooked chicken breast, shredded
1 cup	fat free refried beans
½ tsp.	ground cumin
	guacamole, sour cream, shredded cheese, shredded lettuce, salsa, or pico de gallo to garnish

If not using purchased tostadas, preheat oven to 450°F. Bake tortillas for 8 minutes until golden brown and very crisp. If using purchased tostadas, heat at 250°F for 5 minutes to warm. Simmer barbecue sauce and chipotle pepper in a saucepan over medium-low heat for 8 minutes or until sauce is syrupy. Remove from heat and stir in shredded chicken. Mix refried beans with cumin. Just before serving, heat beans in microwave for 30 seconds on medium. Stir well to make sure beans are warm through. Spread each tostada with ¼ cup refried beans. Top with ½ cup shredded chicken mixture. Garnish as desired with guacamole, sour cream, shredded cheese, lettuce, salsa, and pico de gallo.

MOPS Mom: Honey Lemonade Chicken

■ *Angie Jones, Indian Land, South Carolina* ■

6 oz.	frozen lemonade or limeade concentrate, thawed
¼ cup	honey
1 Tbs.	Worcestershire sauce
1 Tbs.	olive oil
4	boneless, skinless chicken breasts, pounded thin

Preheat oven to 325°F, and spray a 9 x 13 baking dish with nonstick cooking spray. To easily mix the liquids without the lemonade thickening the honey, place the baking dish with the 4 liquid ingredients in the oven while it is preheating, then remove dish and stir ingredients together. Place chicken in dish, and turn to coat. Bake for 15–20 minutes, until chicken is no longer pink.

Complete the meal by serving over white or brown rice with Easy Green Beans.

MOPS Mom: Chicken Stuffed Shells

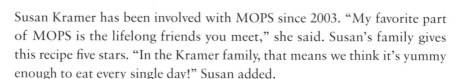

■ *Susan Kramer, West Jefferson, Ohio* ■

Susan Kramer has been involved with MOPS since 2003. "My favorite part of MOPS is the lifelong friends you meet," she said. Susan's family gives this recipe five stars. "In the Kramer family, that means we think it's yummy enough to eat every single day!" Susan added.

Susan and her husband, Aaron, are the parents of Adam, Riah, and Mara.

1 (6 oz.) box	stuffing, prepared according to pkg. directions
2 cups	cooked chicken, diced
¾ cup	mayonnaise
2 (10.75 oz.) cans	cream of chicken soup
1 soup can	water
¾ cup	cheddar cheese, shredded
12 oz.	jumbo pasta shells, cooked according to pkg. directions

Preheat oven to 350°F. Spray a 9 x 13 baking dish with nonstick cooking spray. Combine stuffing, chicken, and mayonnaise. Fill pasta shells with stuffing mixture. Place filled shells in baking dish. Whisk cream of chicken soup with water and pour over shells. Cover with foil and bake for 40 minutes. Sprinkle cheese over top and bake uncovered another 10 minutes or until cheese melts.

Complete the meal with Broccoli and Green Bean Duo.

Chicken Tenders with Apricot Sauce

⅔ cup	apricot preserves
2 Tbs.	soy sauce
2 tsp.	ketchup
1 Tbs.	fresh ginger, peeled and minced
1 Tbs.	fresh lemon juice
2 cups	panko (Japanese style bread crumbs)
2 tsp.	salt
1 tsp.	black pepper
4	boneless, skinless chicken breasts, sliced into 4 tenders each
3	eggs, beaten
	vegetable oil for frying

Combine preserves, soy sauce, ketchup, and ginger in a microwave-safe bowl. Heat on high about 30 seconds and stir in lemon juice. Set aside. Preheat oven to 225°F. Toss panko with salt and pepper in a shallow dish. Heat ½ inch of oil in large skillet over medium-high heat. Dip each chicken tender in beaten egg and then dredge in panko. Place chicken in skillet, careful not to overcrowd. Fry chicken on each side for about 2½ minutes until evenly brown. Keep each batch warm until all chicken is fried. Serve hot with the apricot sauce.

Complete the meal with Baked Sweet Potato Sticks.

Sweet and Sour Chicken

2 Tbs.	vegetable oil
2 cups	boneless, skinless chicken breast, cut into bite-size pieces
½ cup	apricot preserves
2 Tbs.	soy sauce
2 Tbs.	apple cider vinegar
2 Tbs.	fresh ginger, grated
½ cup	roasted cashews, optional
1 cup	white or brown rice, cooked according to pkg. directions
2	green onions, thinly sliced

To freeze this meal, do not add cashews or green onions. When ready to reheat, simply thaw and microwave or gently reheat in a skillet. Add cashews and green onions right before serving.

Heat vegetable oil in large skillet over medium-high heat. Add chicken pieces and cook until no longer pink, stirring occasionally. In a small bowl, whisk together preserves, soy sauce, vinegar, and ginger. Add sauce mixture to chicken and reduce heat to low. Simmer 3 minutes. Add cashews and toss to coat. Serve over cooked rice and sprinkle with green onion.

Complete the meal with Crunchy Asian Slaw.

MOPS Mom: Yummy Zucchini Boats

■ *Laura Casino, Cary, North Carolina* ■

Laura Casino learned to cook from several family members. Her father taught her to create extraordinary meals on a tight budget, while her grandmother stepped in to teach some of the basics, such as boiling an egg or making spaghetti. "My stepmom taught me how to cook like a southerner," she added. "Then I took all of that knowledge and expanded on it and constantly experiment. I take food that looks interesting and try to reinvent it to become tasty and fun!"

Laura discovered this recipe while searching for ways to get her kids to eat vegetables. "I have the hardest time getting my kids to eat veggies—especially if they can see them," Laura said. "However, my kids do eat these and love them! They look cute and are super yummy and easy to make."

Laura and her husband, Chris, are the parents of Loralei, Gavin, and Alexis.

6	med. zucchini
8 oz.	cream cheese, softened
1 lb.	bacon, cooked and chopped
2 cups	mushrooms, diced
2 Tbs.	unsalted butter
½ tsp.	garlic salt
1 lb.	ground chicken, cooked and crumbled

Bring 2 quarts of unsalted water to boil in large saucepan. Add zucchini; cook 6–8 minutes or until fork-tender. Drain. Slice parboiled zucchini in half lengthwise and scoop out centers. Preheat oven to 350°F. Sauté diced mushrooms in butter and garlic salt, and drain. Mix together cream cheese, bacon, mushrooms, and ground chicken. Fill zucchini boats with cream cheese mixture and put on a baking sheet that has been sprayed with nonstick cooking spray. Bake for 20 minutes, until tops are golden brown. Let cool for 5 minutes before serving.

Complete the meal with Berry Salad with Vanilla-Yogurt Dressing.

MOPS Mom: Yummy Chicken Enchiladas

■ *Kim Smelser, Stanwood, Washington* ■

"I have three kiddos all under seven years old, and they all love this dish," Kim said. "And I almost always make this to take to families that have a new baby. Word gets around and if by chance I bring something else they are a bit disappointed. It's so easy and yummy!"

1 sm.	white onion, chopped
2 Tbs.	unsalted butter
4	boneless, skinless chicken breasts, cooked and cubed
6 oz.	cream cheese (can use reduced fat)
½ cup	sliced black olives, optional
12 sm.	flour tortillas
1 cup	whipping cream or half-and-half (fat free works fine)
1½ cups	Monterey Jack or your favorite Mexican blend cheese, shredded

Preheat oven to 350°F. Spray a 9 x 13 baking dish with nonstick cooking spray. In a large skillet, sauté onion in melted butter until softened. Add chicken and heat through. Remove from heat and add cream cheese and black olives, if desired. Stir well to combine. Spoon mixture evenly into center of tortillas and roll into enchiladas. Place in baking dish. When finished, pour cream over enchiladas. Sprinkle with cheese. Bake for about 20–25 minutes, until cheese is melted and enchiladas are slightly browned.

Complete the meal with Refried Black Beans.

MOPS Favorite: Parmesan Chicken

1	garlic clove, minced
½ cup	unsalted butter, melted
1 cup	dried Italian bread crumbs
⅓ cup	Parmesan cheese, grated
¼ tsp.	garlic salt
⅛ tsp.	ground black pepper
2 lbs.	boneless, skinless chicken, cut into chunks

Preheat oven to 450°F. In a small bowl, combine minced garlic with melted butter. In another bowl mix together bread crumbs, Parmesan cheese, garlic salt, and pepper. Dip chicken pieces into garlic butter, then into crumb mixture to coat. Place coated chicken pieces on a 9 x 13 baking dish lightly sprayed with cooking spray. Try to leave a little room between each piece. Drizzle with remaining garlic butter and bake uncovered 15 minutes, or until chicken is cooked through and juices run clear.

Complete the meal with spaghetti marinara and Italian Salad.

Chicken Penne Pasta

12 oz.	penne pasta
1 (14 oz.) can	chicken broth
3	boneless, skinless chicken breasts, cut into 1-inch pieces
½ tsp.	garlic powder
8 oz.	low fat cream cheese, cut into pieces
1 (10 oz.) pkg.	frozen spinach, thawed and squeezed dry
15	cherry or grape tomatoes Parmesan cheese, grated

To freeze, place cooked pasta and chicken mixture in a freezer-safe casserole dish. Top with Parmesan. Wrap tightly in plastic wrap and freeze up to 3 months. To heat, thaw in refrigerator overnight. Remove plastic wrap, cover with foil, and bake at 350°F for 35 minutes. Remove foil and continue baking for 15 more minutes.

Cook pasta according to package directions. Drain and place in large bowl. Cover to keep warm.

Pour half of the chicken broth into a large skillet and heat over medium-high heat until simmering. Add chicken and cook until no longer pink in center, about 10 minutes. Add garlic powder and cream cheese. Stir until cream cheese melts. Add remaining chicken broth, spinach, and tomatoes. Cook for about 10 minutes, stirring occasionally. Sauce will thicken slightly and tomatoes will soften. Add sauce to cooked pasta. Toss well. Serve immediately, topped with grated Parmesan cheese.

Complete the meal with Broccoli Ramen Salad.

Chicken Dijon Pasta and Broccoli

1 lb.	rigatoni or other medium pasta, uncooked
8 oz.	boneless, skinless chicken breast, cut into 1-inch pieces
½ tsp.	salt
¼ tsp.	freshly ground black pepper
2	garlic cloves, minced
3	broccoli florets
1 lg.	red bell pepper, cut into short, thin strips
½ cup	low sodium chicken broth
1 (12 oz.) can	low fat evaporated milk, divided
1 Tbs.	cornstarch
3 Tbs.	Dijon mustard

Prepare pasta according to package directions. Drain and cover to keep warm. Meanwhile, season chicken with salt, pepper, and garlic. Coat a large nonstick skillet with cooking spray and heat over medium-high heat. Add chicken and stir-fry 4–5 minutes or until chicken is cooked through and juices run clear. Remove chicken from skillet and place in a medium bowl. Add broccoli, bell pepper, and chicken broth to skillet. Cover; simmer over medium heat 5–6 minutes or until vegetables are crisp-tender. Transfer to bowl with chicken. In a small bowl, combine ¼ cup evaporated milk with cornstarch, mixing until smooth. Add to skillet with remaining milk; bring to a boil, stirring constantly. Reduce heat; stir in mustard. Stir in reserved chicken mixture, and heat through. Toss pasta with chicken mixture and serve immediately with additional freshly ground pepper, if desired.

Complete the meal with Honey Berry Salad.

Chinese Chicken Noodles

8 oz.	udon noodles or linguine
2	boneless, skinless chicken breast halves, cut crosswise into thin strips
1 Tbs.	cornstarch
	salt and pepper to taste
2 Tbs.	vegetable oil, divided
1 sm.	red onion, halved and thinly sliced
2	garlic cloves, thinly sliced
½ head (1 lb.)	Napa cabbage, thinly shredded
2 cups	frozen shelled edamame
2 Tbs.	rice vinegar
2 Tbs.	soy sauce

Cook noodles according to package instructions. Drain and keep warm. Meanwhile, in a medium bowl, toss chicken with cornstarch. Season with salt and pepper. In a large nonstick skillet, heat 1 tablespoon oil over medium-high heat. Cook chicken in 2 batches, until light brown on the outside and juices no longer run pink, 2–4 minutes. Transfer to a plate. Add remaining tablespoon oil to skillet and add onion and garlic. Cook, stirring frequently, until softened, 1–3 minutes. Add cabbage and cook, stirring frequently, until tender, 2–4 minutes. Add edamame, vinegar, soy sauce, chicken, and noodles. Cook, tossing, until noodles and edamame are warmed through, about 3 minutes.

Slow Cooker Jambalaya

2 lbs.	boneless, skinless chicken breasts
1 lb.	smoked sausage, cut into 2-inch slices
1 lg.	onion, chopped
1 lg.	green bell pepper, seeded and chopped
3 stalks	celery, chopped
1 (28 oz.) can	diced tomatoes, undrained
3	garlic cloves, minced
2 cups	chicken broth

1 Tbs.   Cajun or Creole spice mix
1 tsp.   dried thyme
1 tsp.   dried oregano
1 lb.   large shrimp, peeled and deveined
1¾ cups long-grain white rice, uncooked
         fresh parsley, chopped, to garnish

Combine chicken, sausage, onion, green pepper, celery, tomatoes, garlic, chicken broth, spice mix, thyme, and oregano in a large (5-quart) slow cooker. Cook on low for 5 hours. Add shrimp and rice; cook on high for 30 more minutes. Sprinkle with chopped parsley, if desired.

Italian Chicken

½ lb.   rigatoni pasta
1 tsp.   olive oil
2   boneless, skinless chicken breast halves, halved horizontally
         salt and pepper to taste
3 cups   Alfredo sauce
¼ cup   oil-packed sun-dried tomatoes, drained and thinly sliced
½ cup   provolone cheese, shredded
½ cup   Parmesan cheese, finely grated

Preheat oven to 400°F. Spray a 2-quart baking dish with cooking spray. In a large pot of boiling salted water, cook pasta 3 minutes short of package directions, so that pasta is still just a tad chewy. Drain pasta and set aside. In a large nonstick skillet, heat oil over medium-high heat. Season chicken with salt and pepper; cook until juices run clear, 3–5 minutes per side. Halve each piece lengthwise, then thinly slice crosswise. In a large pot, heat Alfredo sauce over medium heat. Add tomatoes; cook 1 minute. Remove from heat and stir in provolone and ¼ cup Parmesan. Add chicken and pasta; season with salt and pepper. Place pasta mixture in baking dish and sprinkle with remaining Parmesan cheese. Bake, uncovered, until top is golden and bubbling, about 25 minutes. Let stand 5 minutes before serving.

Complete the meal with Broccoli and Green Bean Duo.

Buttermilk Chicken

¼ cup	unsalted butter
4	boneless, skinless chicken breasts
½ tsp.	salt
½ tsp.	pepper
1½ cups	buttermilk, divided
¾ cup	all-purpose flour
1 (10¾ oz.) can	cream of mushroom soup, undiluted
	white or brown rice

Preheat oven to 425°F. Melt butter in a 9 x 13 casserole dish that has been sprayed with cooking spray. Sprinkle chicken with salt and pepper. Dip chicken in ½ cup buttermilk and dredge in flour. Arrange chicken in baking dish. Bake for 15 minutes. Turn chicken over and bake 10 more minutes. Meanwhile, stir together remaining 1 cup of buttermilk and cream of mushroom soup. Pour over chicken, cover with aluminum foil, and bake 10 more minutes. Serve over white or brown rice.

Complete the meal with Updated Green Bean Casserole.

Whole Wheat Cracker Chicken Nuggets

4	boneless, skinless chicken breasts
2 cups	buttermilk
1 sleeve	whole wheat crackers, crushed into crumbs

Nuggets freeze well after coating in crumbs. Bake straight from freezer; just add 5 minutes of cooking time.

Place chicken breasts 2 at a time into a large resealable bag. Seal tightly. Pound with meat mallet or rolling pin until flattened slightly. Cut each breast into 4–5 nuggets. Place chicken nuggets into another large resealable bag, pour in buttermilk, and seal tightly. Place in refrigerator at least 6 hours or overnight. Preheat oven to 425°F. Place cracker crumbs on a shallow plate. Remove each chicken nugget from buttermilk, allowing excess buttermilk to drip off, and dip in crumbs. Coat well. Place on a baking sheet sprayed with cooking spray. Bake for 15–20 minutes, depending on size of nuggets.

Complete the meal with Southwest Creamed Corn or Mashed Potatoes with Fresh Corn.

Chicken Teriyaki

4 (4 oz.)	boneless, skinless chicken breast halves
½ cup	soy sauce
⅓ cup	brown sugar, packed
1 Tbs.	apple cider vinegar
⅓ cup	pineapple juice
1 tsp.	fresh ginger, grated
1 tsp.	garlic, minced

You can also grill the chicken, if desired.

Place chicken in large resealable bag. In small bowl, stir together soy sauce, brown sugar, vinegar, pineapple juice, ginger, and garlic. Pour mixture over chicken. Seal bag and marinate in refrigerator at least 3 hours and up to 8 hours. Shake chicken in bag occasionally. Preheat oven broiler. Remove chicken from bag and discard marinade. Place chicken on broiler pan or cookie sheet that has been sprayed with cooking spray. Broil chicken 6 inches from heat for 6 minutes. Turn chicken over and broil 5 minutes more or until chicken is no longer pink.

Complete the meal: serve over rice with Broccoli and Cashew Stir-Fry.

MOPS Favorite: Chicken and Dumplings

2 (14½ oz.) cans	chicken broth
⅛ tsp.	pepper
2 cups	cooked chicken breast, shredded
1 cup	buttermilk baking mix
⅓ cup	milk

Pour broth into a Dutch oven or large, heavy pot. Bring to a boil. Reduce heat; simmer, uncovered. Add pepper and chicken. For dumplings, combine biscuit mix and milk. Drop by tablespoons onto simmering broth. Cover and simmer for 10–15 minutes or until a toothpick inserted into a dumpling comes out clean. Do not lift cover while simmering.

Complete the meal with Apple Cider Turnips or Carrot Coins.

Roasted Chicken Lasagna

9	whole wheat or regular lasagna noodles, uncooked
20 oz.	refrigerated light Alfredo sauce
3 Tbs.	lemon juice
½ tsp.	black pepper
3 cups	chopped, cooked chicken
1 (10 oz.) pkg.	frozen chopped spinach, thawed and squeezed dry
1 cup	roasted red peppers, drained and chopped
½ cup	provolone cheese, shredded
¼ cup	Parmesan cheese, grated

Preheat oven to 325°F. Cook noodles according to package directions. Drain. Meanwhile, in a bowl combine Alfredo sauce, lemon juice, and black pepper. Stir in chicken, spinach, and red peppers. Lightly coat a 9 x 13 baking dish with nonstick cooking spray. Arrange 3 noodles in bottom of dish. Top with one third of chicken mixture. Repeat layers twice. Cover; bake for 45–55 minutes or until heated through. Uncover; sprinkle with cheese. Bake, uncovered, 5 more minutes or until cheese is melted. Let stand 15 minutes before serving. Serves 8. Complete the meal with Glazed Brussels Sprouts with Bacon.

Slow Cooker Indian Chicken

2 lbs.	boneless, skinless chicken breasts
2 Tbs.	garam masala
½ tsp.	salt
½ tsp.	turmeric
½ cup	all-purpose flour
1 Tbs.	vegetable oil
1 lg.	yellow onion, chopped
6	garlic cloves, minced
2 Tbs.	fresh ginger, grated
1 (28 oz.) can	crushed tomatoes
1 cup	frozen peas
½ cup	light sour cream
¼ cup	fresh cilantro, chopped, if desired

Garam masala can be found in the spice aisle of your grocery store.

Place chicken in a large bowl. In a small bowl, mix garam masala, salt, and turmeric. Add ½ teaspoon of this spice mixture to the flour. Mix well. Coat chicken breasts in flour mixture.

Heat oil in a large skillet over medium-high heat. Add chicken and brown, about 3–4 minutes per side. Add onion, garlic, and ginger and cook 2 minutes. Place chicken, onion, garlic, and ginger in bottom of a slow cooker. Add tomatoes, peas, and remaining spice mixture. Stir well.

Cook on high for 4–6 hours or on low for 8–10 hours. Just before serving, remove chicken from slow cooker and add sour cream. Stir well. Return chicken to heat through. Serve over rice and garnish with cilantro, if desired.

Asian Chicken with Green Beans

1 Tbs.	cornstarch
¼ cup	light brown sugar
¼ cup	soy sauce
¼ cup	white or rice wine vinegar
1 Tbs.	vegetable oil
1¼ lbs.	boneless, skinless chicken breast, cut into 1-inch pieces
2	bell peppers (any color), diced
½ lb.	fresh green beans, trimmed and halved
5	green onions, thinly sliced
2 Tbs.	fresh ginger, peeled and minced
3	garlic cloves, minced
1 cup	white, brown, or Jasmine rice, cooked according to pkg. directions
2 Tbs.	roasted peanuts, chopped, optional

Whisk together cornstarch, sugar, soy sauce, and vinegar. Set aside. In a large skillet or wok, heat oil over high heat. Add chicken, bell peppers, and green beans and cook, stirring, for about 5 minutes. Add green onions, ginger, and garlic and cook, stirring, for 3–4 more minutes. Whisk the soy sauce mixture again, and pour into skillet. Cook and stir for 3 minutes, until sauce starts to thicken. Remove from heat. When ready to serve, spoon mixture over rice and top with peanuts, if desired.

Easy Roasted Turkey Breast

1¼ cups	coarse salt
1 cup	light brown sugar, packed
1 gal.	water
1 (5 lb.)	whole turkey breast, thawed

In a large stockpot, dissolve salt and sugar in water. Place turkey in salt water. Put a heavy plate over turkey to keep it from floating. Refrigerate 8 hours. Remove turkey from salt water and rinse. Pat dry. Preheat oven to 350°F. Place turkey on a baking sheet with sides and cook 1½ hours or until internal temperature reaches 165°F. Let rest 10 minutes before slicing.

Complete the meal with Bacon Squash Sauté and Artichoke Rice.

Sesame Beef and Asparagus

1¼ lbs.	top sirloin, thinly sliced against grain
	salt and pepper to taste
3 Tbs.	toasted sesame seeds
3 Tbs.	canola oil
1 Tbs.	sesame oil
1 sm.	red onion, thinly sliced
2 cups	fresh asparagus spears, trimmed and cut into 2-inch pieces
½ cup	water
¼ cup	hoisin sauce
	rice

Sprinkle beef with salt and pepper. Coat with sesame seeds. Heat canola and sesame oils in wok or large skillet over high heat. Stir-fry onion about 1 minute, then add asparagus and stir-fry 2 more minutes. Add beef and stir-fry until browned, about 2 minutes. Reduce heat to medium, and add water and hoisin sauce. Cook, stirring, 2 minutes, until sauce has thickened a little and is coating beef and vegetables. Serve over rice.

Beef Fondue

¼ cup soy sauce
3 Tbs. Worcestershire sauce
1 garlic clove, minced
2 lbs. beef tenderloin, cut
into 1-inch cubes
peanut or vegetable oil
barbecue sauce, green goddess salad dressing, and
horseradish sour cream sauce for serving, if desired

Fondue involves working with hot oil, so it is best to save this recipe for families with older children.

In a large resealable plastic bag, combine soy sauce, Worcestershire sauce, and garlic; add meat. Seal bag and turn to coat; refrigerate for 4 hours, turning occasionally. Drain and discard marinade. Pat meat dry with paper towels. Using 1 fondue pot for every 6 people, heat 2–3 cups oil in each pot to 375°F. Use fondue forks to cook meat in oil until it reaches desired doneness (30 seconds for rare, 45 seconds for medium-rare). Serve with assorted prepared sauces. Serves 4–6.

Complete the meal with Gruyère Potato Gratin and Oven-Roasted Green Beans.

Easy Beef Stroganoff

12 oz.	egg noodles
2 Tbs.	olive oil, divided
1 lb.	flank steak, thinly sliced
	salt and pepper
1 sm.	yellow onion, thinly sliced
1	green or red bell pepper, thinly sliced, if desired
1 (4–5 oz.) jar	sliced mushrooms, drained
1 cup	sour cream or Greek plain yogurt
2 Tbs.	steak sauce
2 tsp.	Worcestershire sauce

Cook noodles according to package directions. Meanwhile, heat 1 tablespoon oil in a large skillet over medium-high heat. Season the steak with ¼ teaspoon each salt and pepper, or to taste.

In 2 batches, cook the steak until browned, about 1 minute per side. Transfer to a plate.

Return skillet to medium heat and add remaining tablespoon of oil. Add onion and bell pepper, if desired; cook until softened, 6–8 minutes. Add mushrooms and beef and cook until warmed through, about 2 minutes. In a small bowl, combine sour cream, steak sauce, and Worcestershire sauce, and stir into beef and mushrooms. Serve over noodles.

Complete the meal with Maple Roasted Butternut Squash.

Spicy Pot Roast

1 (3–5 lb.)	chuck or arm roast, trimmed of excess fat
2 Tbs.	vegetable oil
1 lb.	carrots, peeled and sliced
4–5 med.	white or sweet potatoes (if using white, do not have to peel), cubed
2 stalks	celery, chopped
1	bay leaf
½ cup	brown sugar, firmly packed
½ cup	cider vinegar
¼ cup	soy sauce
¼ tsp.	salt
⅛ tsp.	pepper
1 cup	water

Preheat oven to 325°F. Heat oil in skillet over high heat; add meat and brown all sides. Place roast in pan or Dutch oven with carrots, potatoes, celery, and bay leaf. Mix together brown sugar, vinegar, soy sauce, salt, and pepper. Add water and pour over roast. Cover tightly with heavy-duty foil or lid. Cook for 3–4 hours, depending on size of roast. Remove meat and vegetables and make gravy with the drippings, if desired.

To make gravy, place drippings in a saucepan over medium-high heat. Add 2 tablespoons of cornstarch to ¼ cup cool water and whisk to make a thin paste. Pour into pan drippings, whisking constantly. As gravy thickens, slowly whisk in 2 cups of hot beef broth (or milk for a white gravy). Whisk until thickened. Add salt and pepper to taste.

Complete the meal with Potluck Marinated Vegetable Salad.

Beef Fajitas

8 (6 in.)	flour tortillas
1½ lbs.	flank steak
½ tsp.	salt
¾ tsp.	black pepper, divided
2 Tbs.	vegetable oil, divided
2	bell peppers (any color), ribs and seeds removed and thinly sliced
1 sm.	white onion, thinly sliced lengthwise
1 tsp.	ground cumin
½ tsp.	coarse salt
1 Tbs.	lemon or lime juice
	shredded cheese, sour cream, salsa, or other desired toppings

Preheat oven to 250°F. Wrap tortillas in foil and place in oven to warm. Season flank steak with salt and ½ teaspoon pepper. Heat 1 tablespoon oil in large skillet over medium-high heat. Add steak and cook 5 minutes on each side for medium-rare. Do not overcook. Remove steak from skillet and place on cutting surface. Cover meat loosely with aluminum foil while preparing onions and peppers. Heat remaining 1 tablespoon oil in skillet over medium-high heat. Add peppers, onions, cumin, salt, and remaining ¼ teaspoon pepper. Sauté, stirring occasionally, until vegetables are tender, about 5 minutes. Add lemon or lime juice and toss to combine. Remove skillet from heat. Thinly slice flank steak against the grain and serve with tortillas, onions, peppers, and any other desired toppings.

Orange, Honey, and Chipotle Flank Steak

2 cups	orange juice
5 Tbs.	honey
¼ cup	soy sauce
2 tsp.	chipotle chiles in adobo sauce, minced
2 lbs.	flank steak

This sauce is also great over pork, shrimp, and chicken.

Combine orange juice, honey, and soy sauce in a saucepan and boil until reduced by half, about 30 minutes. Stir in chiles. Be careful not to overcook, or glaze will burn. Heat charcoal or gas grill to high heat. Grill flank steak 3–4 inches from heat for 4–5 minutes per side for medium-rare and 6–7 minutes per side for medium, brushing glaze over both sides of steak while grilling.

Complete the meal with Chile-Roasted Sweet Potatoes.

Balsamic Filet Mignon

4 (4 oz.)	beef tenderloin steaks
¼ tsp.	salt
¼ tsp.	black pepper
2 tsp.	minced garlic
⅛ tsp.	crushed red pepper
3 Tbs.	cooking sherry
2 Tbs.	soy sauce
1 Tbs.	balsamic vinegar
2 tsp.	honey

Season steaks with salt and pepper. Spray a large skillet with nonstick cooking spray and heat over medium-high heat. Once skillet warms, add steak. Cook for 3 minutes on each side or until desired degree of doneness. Remove steaks from skillet and cover loosely with foil to keep warm. Add garlic and red pepper to skillet and sauté for 30 seconds. Add sherry and bring to a boil. Add soy sauce, vinegar, and honey. Return to a boil, stirring occasionally. Reduce heat and simmer for 1 minute. Serve sauce with steaks.

Complete the meal with Goat Cheese Mashed Potatoes and Winter Pear Salad.

Family-Style Tamale Casserole

1 lb.	ground beef
1 (15 oz.) can	ranchero beans
1 (16 oz.) jar	medium salsa
1 (12 oz.) box	corn bread mix
1	egg
1⅓ cups	buttermilk
¼ cup	sugar, optional
6 Tbs.	unsalted butter, melted
1 (4 oz.) can	mild green chiles, diced

Preheat oven to 400°F. In a large sauté pan, crumble and brown meat. Drain and return to stove. Add beans and salsa, and stir to combine. Simmer 6 minutes. Let cool slightly, then spoon into a 9 x 13 baking dish. Prepare corn bread batter according to package directions, using egg, buttermilk, sugar, butter, and chiles. Carefully spoon over top of beef mixture, and smooth with back of spoon. Bake 15–20 minutes or until corn bread is lightly brown and filling is bubbling.

Complete the meal with a simple tossed green salad.

Miniature Meatloaves

1 Tbs.	olive oil
1 cup	yellow onion, chopped
1 cup	green pepper, chopped
1 tsp.	fresh thyme
1 tsp.	salt
1 tsp.	freshly ground black pepper
2 Tbs.	Worcestershire sauce
1 Tbs.	tomato paste
1½ lbs.	ground beef
½ cup	plain dry bread crumbs
2 lg.	eggs, beaten
½ cup	ketchup

Preheat the oven to 350°F. Heat olive oil in a medium sauté pan. Add onions, green pepper, thyme, salt, and pepper and cook over medium-low heat, stirring occasionally, for 8–10 minutes, until onions are translucent but not brown. Remove pan from heat, and add Worcestershire sauce and tomato paste. Allow to cool slightly. In a large bowl, combine ground beef, onion mixture, bread crumbs, and eggs, and mix by hand until the ingredients are thoroughly combined. Place foil liners in a 12-cup muffin pan and shape individual portions of meatloaf to fit each muffin cup. Spread about a tablespoon of ketchup on the top of each portion. Bake for 40–45 minutes, until the internal temperature is 155–160° and the meatloaves are cooked through. Serve hot.

Complete the meal with Chipotle Potatoes and Updated Green Bean Casserole.

Cajun Flank Steak with Creamed Corn

2 Tbs.	unsalted butter
1 sm.	yellow onion, chopped
4 cups	fresh corn kernels
1 cup	half-and-half
½ tsp.	salt
¼ tsp.	pepper
1½ lbs.	flank steak, divided in half
2 tsp.	Cajun seasoning

Preheat oven broiler. Melt butter in a medium saucepan over medium-high heat. Add onion and cook until softened, about 4–5 minutes. Add corn, half-and-half, salt, and pepper. Heat thoroughly and set aside to keep warm. Season steak with Cajun seasoning and additional salt and pepper, if desired. Place on foil-lined baking sheet and broil 3–4 minutes per side. Remove from oven and let sit 5 minutes before slicing against the grain. Serve steak and corn together.

Complete the meal with Strawberry Spinach Salad.

Spicy Beef Stir-Fry

1 Tbs.	vegetable oil
1 lb.	flank steak, sliced thinly against the grain
	salt and pepper to taste
½ lb.	sugar snap peas
2 med.	carrots, thinly sliced
1	shallot, diced
1	garlic clove, minced
⅓ cup	red or green pepper jelly
8 oz.	lo mein or spaghetti noodles, cooked according to pkg. directions

Heat oil in a large skillet over medium-high heat. Season beef with salt and pepper. Cook in skillet for 4 minutes total, flipping after 2 minutes. Remove beef and keep warm. Add sugar snap peas, carrots, shallot, and garlic to skillet. Cook, stirring, for 4 minutes. Return beef to skillet and stir in jelly. Cook 1 more minute, stirring. Serve with noodles.

Quick Tortellini Bake

1 lb.	lean ground beef
1 sm.	yellow onion, finely chopped
3 tsp.	minced garlic
1 (28 oz.) can	crushed tomatoes
6 leaves	fresh basil, torn into pieces
½ tsp.	salt
½ tsp.	black pepper
2 lbs.	cheese-filled tortellini, cooked according to pkg. directions
½ cup	Parmesan cheese, grated
1 cup	mozzarella cheese, shredded

Cook ground beef in large skillet over medium-high heat until brown, 6–7 minutes. Drain any grease, and return to heat. Add onion and garlic and cook until tender, about 5 minutes. Add tomatoes, basil, salt, and pepper. Simmer until slightly thickened, about 7 minutes. Add cooked tortellini to skillet and toss to coat. Transfer to a large casserole dish and sprinkle with both cheeses. Place under oven broiler to brown, about 1 minute.

Complete the meal with Herbed Spaghetti Squash.

MOPS Favorite: Easy Oven Brisket

1 (5 lb.)	beef brisket
2 Tbs.	liquid smoke
2 tsp.	onion salt
2 tsp.	salt
2 tsp.	black pepper
1 tsp.	garlic salt
2 tsp.	celery salt
2 tsp.	Worcestershire sauce

Make a paste of all ingredients excluding brisket. Rub paste over all surfaces and edges of brisket. Place meat fat side up on a large piece of heavy-duty foil. Wrap and seal well, folding edges of foil as securely as possible. Refrigerate in a baking pan with sides for 12–24 hours. Preheat oven to 250°F. Take brisket directly from refrigerator and bake in foil for 8 hours. Brisket will be very tender.

Complete the meal with Molasses Barbecue Beans and Lightened Creamed Corn.

Slow Cooker Vegetarian Lasagna

2 (28 oz.) cans	diced tomatoes, drained
3	garlic cloves, finely chopped
¼ cup	fresh oregano, chopped
½ tsp.	salt
¾ tsp.	pepper, divided
16 oz.	ricotta or cottage cheese
½ cup	fresh flat-leaf parsley, chopped
½ cup	Parmesan cheese, grated
12 oz.	lasagna noodles, uncooked
1 bunch	Swiss chard, tough stems removed, torn into large pieces (approx. 7 cups)
12 oz.	mozzarella cheese, shredded

Hint: your family will never miss the meat—the Swiss chard cooks down and tastes delicious!

In a medium bowl, combine tomatoes, garlic, oregano, salt, and ½ teaspoon pepper. In another bowl, combine ricotta, parsley, Parmesan, and remaining ¼ teaspoon pepper. Spoon ⅓ cup of the tomato mixture into the bottom of a slow cooker. Top with a single layer of noodles, breaking them to fit as necessary. Add half the Swiss chard. Dollop with a third of the ricotta mixture and a third of the remaining tomato mixture. Sprinkle with 1 cup of the mozzarella. Add another layer of noodles and repeat layers of other ingredients. Finish with a third layer of noodles and the remaining ricotta mixture, tomato mixture, and mozzarella. Set the slow cooker to low and cook, covered, until the noodles are tender, about 2 hours.

Complete the meal with Italian Salad and garlic bread.

MOPS Mom: One-Pot Spaghetti

■ *Kerri Scibelli, Dallas, Texas* ■

As a wife to Jason and a mom of young twin boys, Kerri Scibelli needs recipes that are easy, quick, and full of flavor. She found this recipe in the newspaper almost ten years ago as a newlywed learning to cook, and it's been a weekly favorite in her house ever since.

"I like MOPS for several reasons, but mostly, it's a welcome respite and time with other like-minded moms," Kerri said. "And hearing a speaker and doing a fun craft just rounds out the day. It's something I look forward to!"

Kerri also said that even though her boys, Sutton and Fisher, are still a bit young to do the crafts or understand the Bible verses, she loves that they get a chance to play and socialize with other kids their age.

½ lb.	ground beef or bulk pork sausage
1 cup	sliced fresh mushrooms, or 1 6-oz. jar sliced mushrooms, drained
½ cup	yellow onion, chopped
1	garlic clove, minced
1 (14 oz.) can	chicken or beef broth
1¾ cups	water
1 (6 oz.) can	tomato paste
1 tsp.	dried Italian seasoning
¼ tsp.	black pepper
6 oz.	dried spaghetti, broken into pieces
¼ cup	Parmesan cheese, grated

In a large saucepan, cook ground beef, fresh mushrooms (if using), onion, and garlic until meat is brown and onion is tender. Drain. Stir in canned mushrooms (if using), broth, water, tomato paste, Italian seasoning, and pepper. Bring to a boil. Add broken spaghetti, a little at a time, stirring constantly. Return to boiling; reduce heat. Boil gently, uncovered, for 17–20 minutes or until spaghetti is tender and sauce is desired consistency, stirring frequently. Serve with Parmesan cheese. Makes 4 servings.

Complete the meal with Easy Green Beans.

MOPS Mom: Cheesy Italian Tenderloins

■ *Sarah Clark, Raleigh, North Carolina* ■

4	beef tenderloin steaks, 1-inch thick
1 Tbs.	olive or vegetable oil
¼ tsp.	garlic salt
1	Roma tomato, seeded and chopped
¼ cup	fresh basil leaves, chopped
¼ cup	mozzarella cheese, shredded

Preheat oven to broil. Brush each side of beef with oil and sprinkle with garlic salt. Place beef on rack in broiler pan 4–6 inches from heat. Broil 12 minutes, turning once halfway through. Remove broiler pan from oven. Sprinkle beef with tomato, basil, and cheese. Return to oven and broil 1 minute or just until cheese begins to melt. Serve immediately.

Complete the meal with Rosemary New Potatoes and Broccoli Ramen Salad.

Coconut Beef Curry

2 Tbs.	vegetable oil
1 lb.	beef sirloin, sliced into thin strips
	salt and pepper to taste
1	red onion, thinly sliced
2	red or orange bell peppers, seeded and thinly sliced
⅓ cup	water
1 Tbs.	red curry paste
1 (14 oz.) can	unsweetened coconut milk
1 cup	fresh basil leaves
1 Tbs.	fresh lime juice
8 oz.	angel hair pasta, cooked according to pkg. directions

Heat 1 tablespoon of oil in a large skillet over medium-high heat. Sprinkle beef with salt and pepper. Add half to skillet. Do not stir; allow beef to brown for 2 minutes per side. Remove beef and keep warm; repeat with remaining oil and beef. Add onion, peppers, and water to skillet, and cook for 3 minutes, stirring occasionally. Add curry paste; cook 1 minute while stirring constantly. Return beef and any accumulated juices to skillet. Add coconut milk and simmer until sauce is slightly thickened, about 4 minutes. Remove from heat. Stir in basil and lime juice. Add salt and pepper to taste. Serve over angel hair pasta.

MOPS Favorite: Mexican Lasagna

1 lb.	ground beef or turkey
1 pkg.	taco seasoning
1 cup	water
12 (6 in.)	corn tortillas
1 cup	salsa
1 (8 oz.) can	tomato sauce
1 (15 oz.) can	kernel corn, drained
1 (4 oz.) can	sliced black olives, drained
1 (4 oz.) can	diced mild green chiles, drained
2 cups	Monterey Jack cheese, shredded

Preheat oven to 375°F. Brown meat; add taco seasoning and water. Cook until thickened. Spray a 9 x 13 pan with nonstick cooking spray. Place 6 tortillas in pan, overlapping as needed to fit. Mix salsa and tomato sauce; set aside. Top tortillas with half the meat, corn, olives, and chiles. Pour half of salsa mixture over this, and sprinkle with 1 cup cheese. Repeat layers, finishing with cheese. Bake 30 minutes. Serves 6–8.

Complete the meal with Berry Salad with Vanilla-Yogurt Dressing.

Easy Spaghetti and Meatballs

¼ cup	finely grated Parmesan cheese, plus more for serving
¼ cup	fresh parsley, chopped
2	garlic cloves, minced
1 lg.	egg, slightly beaten
1 tsp.	salt
1 tsp.	black pepper
1 lb.	ground chuck
¼ cup	plain dried bread crumbs
1 Tbs.	olive oil
1 (28 oz.) can	crushed tomatoes in puree
¾ lb.	spaghetti

Set a large pot of salted water to boil. In a bowl, combine Parmesan cheese, parsley, garlic, egg, salt, and pepper. Add beef and bread crumbs; mix gently. Form into 16 balls. In a large, heavy pot, heat oil over medium heat. Add meatballs and cook, turning occasionally, until browned, 8–10 minutes. Add tomatoes; bring to a boil. Reduce to a simmer; cover partially and cook, stirring occasionally, until meatballs are cooked through, 10–12 minutes. Check for taste and add more salt and pepper if desired. (Remember, the Parmesan cheese you sprinkle over the top will also add saltiness.) Meanwhile, cook spaghetti in the large pot of boiling, salted water according to package directions. Drain and return to pot; add meatballs and sauce, and toss gently. Serve with Parmesan cheese.

Complete the meal with Oven-Roasted Green Beans.

Quick Beef and Broccoli Stir-Fry

1½ Tbs.	cornstarch
¼ tsp.	salt
¼ tsp.	black pepper
¾ lb.	sirloin beef tips, thinly sliced against the grain
3 Tbs.	vegetable oil, divided
1 (10 oz.) pkg.	frozen broccoli florets, thawed
3	garlic cloves, chopped
3 Tbs.	soy sauce
⅓ cup	water

Toss together cornstarch, salt, pepper, and beef in a bowl until meat is coated. Heat 2 tablespoons oil in wok over moderately high heat until hot but not smoking, then stir-fry beef until just cooked through, about 1 minute. Transfer beef to another bowl with a slotted spoon and keep warm, loosely covered with foil. Add remaining tablespoon oil to wok along with broccoli and garlic, and stir-fry over moderately high heat until broccoli is just tender and garlic is pale golden, about 2 minutes. Add soy sauce and water and bring to a boil. Return meat to skillet and cook, stirring, until sauce is thickened, about 2 minutes. Serve over rice or lo mein noodles.

Slow Cooker Chipotle Beef Tacos

3 lbs.	beef chuck roast, cut into chunks
1 lg.	white onion, sliced
3	garlic cloves, chopped
2–3 Tbs.	chipotle peppers in adobo sauce, minced (the more you use, the spicier it is)
1 tsp.	ground cumin
1 tsp.	dried oregano
1 tsp.	salt
12 (8 in.)	flour tortillas, warmed
	shredded cabbage, sour cream, salsa, and lime wedges, if desired

Combine beef, onion, garlic, chipotles, cumin, oregano, and salt in slow cooker. Cover and cook on low for 7–8 hours or on high for 3½–4 hours. Remove beef from cooker, reserving liquid. Shred beef using 2 forks. Strain liquid and add back with the shredded beef. Mix well. To serve, fill tortillas with beef. Serve with shredded cabbage, sour cream, salsa, and lime wedges, if desired.

Complete the meal with Southwest Creamed Corn.

Slow Cooker Short Ribs

⅔ cup	all-purpose flour
1½ tsp.	salt
½ tsp.	pepper
4 lbs.	boneless beef short ribs
¼ cup	unsalted butter
1	yellow onion, chopped
1½ cups	beef broth
¾ cup	red wine vinegar
½ cup	packed brown sugar
½ cup	chili sauce
¼ cup	ketchup
⅓ cup	Worcestershire sauce
6	garlic cloves, minced
2 tsp.	chili powder

Combine flour, salt, and pepper in a large resealable plastic bag. Add ribs in batches, and shake to coat. Heat a large skillet over medium-high heat, and add butter. When melted, add ribs and brown meat on all sides. Place browned ribs in a large slow cooker. Using the same skillet, brown onions. Add remaining ingredients, and bring to a boil. Pour over ribs in slow cooker. Cover and cook on low for 10 hours, until meat is tender. Serves 8–10.

Complete the meal with Goat Cheese Mashed Potatoes and Winter Pear Salad.

MOPS Mom: Apricot Glazed Pork Chops

■ *Carrie Anderson, Thomaston, Georgia* ■

Carrie Anderson discovered this recipe when she was given a packet of recipes while still in high school. And although she didn't start cooking until after she married her husband, Jason, she quickly learned how to read and follow recipes for her family to enjoy. "I have been making these pork chops for years, and my husband and several friends and family members always request it."

Carrie and Jason are the parents of preschool twins. "I like MOPS because it gives you a way to be with other moms who are going through the same daily struggles and triumphs," Carrie said. "It's also a way to come together and meet new friends."

4	boneless pork chops
	salt and pepper to taste
2 Tbs.	olive oil
½ cup	apricot nectar
¼ cup	soy sauce
¾ cup	apricot preserves
2	garlic cloves, minced
2 cups	white rice, cooked

Salt and pepper pork chops. Heat olive oil in skillet over medium-high heat and brown pork chops on each side. Combine apricot nectar, soy sauce, apricot preserves, and garlic cloves and pour in skillet over chops. Bring to a simmer and cook, covered, until chops are cooked through, about 20 minutes depending on the thickness of your pork chops. Serve over rice with extra juices poured over top.

Complete the meal with Carrot Coins.

MOPS Mom: Slow Cooker Pulled Pork

■ Heidi Johnson, Wake Forest, North Carolina ■

Heidi Johnson grew up in Texas helping her mom in the kitchen. But it wasn't until she left home that she learned how to really cook on her own. "I learned to cook from my mom, a cookbook called *The Joy of Cooking*, and the internet," Heidi said. "My husband, Clay, loves that I like to cook."

Heidi and Clay have a young son, and their second baby is on the way. This favorite recipe is something she created by combining several other recipes into one. "The sauce is my dad's, the spice and mustard rub is from *Cook's Illustrated*, and the rest came from some slow cooker barbecue recipes on the internet."

1 (5–7 lb.)	pork butt
¼ cup	prepared yellow mustard
2 tsp.	liquid smoke
2 Tbs.	ground black pepper
2 Tbs.	smoked (or regular) paprika
2 Tbs.	sugar
2 tsp.	salt
1 tsp.	cayenne pepper
1 cup	beef broth
2 cups	Barbecue Sauce (see below)

Combine mustard and liquid smoke in small bowl; set aside. Combine black pepper, paprika, sugar, salt, and cayenne pepper in second small bowl; set aside. Rub mustard mixture over entire surface of pork, then sprinkle entire surface with spice mixture. Pour broth into slow cooker. Add pork roast with the fatty side up and cover. Cook 12 hours on low. Drain meat juices into a bowl and shred the meat with a fork or tongs. Return shredded meat to slow cooker. Separate fat from meat juices with a fat separator, or place bowl of juices in freezer until fat congeals and can be scooped off the top. Pour 2 cups of Barbecue Sauce on shredded pork, along with 1 cup of meat juices. Cook on low in slow cooker for another hour or until heated through. Serve on hamburger buns with extra barbecue sauce, if desired. Makes 8–10 sandwiches.

Complete the meal with German Potato Salad and Buttermilk Coleslaw.

Barbecue Sauce

¼ cup	ketchup
¾ cup	chunky salsa
½ cup	soy sauce
1 cup	brown sugar
½ tsp.	garlic powder
¼ tsp.	pepper
2 tsp.	parsley

Combine all ingredients in a saucepan. Heat through and simmer 10–15 minutes. Makes a little more than 2 cups. Can store in refrigerator for up to a week.

White Barbecue Sauce

1½ cups	mayonnaise
¼ cup	white wine vinegar
1	garlic clove, minced
1 Tbs.	coarsely ground black pepper
1 Tbs.	spicy brown mustard
1 tsp.	sugar
1 tsp.	salt
2 tsp.	prepared horseradish

This sauce goes great with all grilled meats.

Stir together all ingredients until well blended. Makes about 2 cups. Store in an airtight container in refrigerator up to 1 week.

Honey Mustard Glazed Pork Chops

½ cup	honey
½ cup	Dijon mustard
½ tsp.	red pepper flakes
1 cup	apple juice
4 lbs.	boneless pork loin chops, about 1-inch thick
	salt and pepper to taste

Combine all ingredients except pork, salt, and pepper in a small saucepan. Bring to a boil, then reduce heat and simmer until glaze is thick enough to coat the back of a spoon. Let cool completely. Reserve half of the glaze to serve as dipping sauce. Preheat grill to medium-high heat. Season pork chops with salt and pepper. Brush glaze on 1 side of the chops. Place chops, glaze-side down, on the grill, and quickly brush more glaze on the top side. Grill for 4 minutes, then turn and glaze the other side. Grill for 4 minutes, flip again, and glaze again. Continue glazing and turning the chops for a total cooking time of 12 minutes or until internal temperature reaches 140–45°F. Let rest for 5 minutes before serving with dipping sauce.

Complete the meal with Brown Rice Risotto.

Rosemary Rubbed Pork Tenderloin

1 Tbs.	freshly ground black pepper
2 tsp.	coarse salt
1 Tbs.	dried rosemary (or 3 Tbs. fresh)
2 lg.	garlic cloves, minced
2 (1 lb.)	pork tenderloins
2 Tbs.	olive oil

Combine pepper, salt, rosemary, and garlic and rub all over pork. Let sit 10 minutes. Preheat oven to 400°F. Heat olive oil in a heavy, ovenproof skillet over high heat. Brown pork on all sides in skillet, about 5 minutes total. Place skillet in oven and roast pork for 10 minutes. Turn pork over, and roast 10 more minutes. Remove from oven, and let rest 5 minutes. Serve in slices.

Complete the meal with Cranberry Wild Rice Pilaf.

Korean Pork Ribs

1¼ cups	light brown sugar
1 cup	soy sauce
1 Tbs.	sesame oil
¼ tsp.	crushed red pepper
4	garlic cloves, finely chopped
2 Tbs.	fresh ginger, minced
½ cup	water
3 lbs.	pork baby back ribs
3	green onions, thinly sliced

Whisk together all ingredients except ribs and green onions. Place in a large resealable plastic bag and add ribs. Toss to coat. Refrigerate at least 1 hour and up to overnight, turning occasionally to coat.

Preheat oven to 450°F. Remove ribs from marinade and place, curved side up, on a rimmed, foil-lined baking sheet. Bake for 20 minutes. While baking, heat marinade over medium-high heat, stirring occasionally, until thick and syrupy. This takes about 15 minutes. Baste ribs in oven, and using tongs, flip ribs over and cook 20 more minutes, basting frequently. Ribs should be brown and tender. Transfer ribs to a platter and garnish with green onions.

Complete the meal with Thai Noodle Salad.

Slow Cooker Chinese Pork Shoulder

1 tsp.	five-spice powder
1 tsp.	salt
1 (3 lb.)	pork shoulder, trimmed of excess fat
3 cups	chicken broth
1 cup	soy sauce
¼ cup	dark brown sugar
2 Tbs.	sesame oil
¼ tsp.	crushed red pepper
6	green onions, sliced
6	garlic cloves, minced
2 Tbs.	fresh ginger, grated
	noodles or rice

Combine five-spice powder and salt. Rub all over pork. Pour broth, soy sauce, brown sugar, oil, and red pepper into slow cooker. Stir well. Add pork, onions, garlic, and ginger. Stir well, turning meat over a few times to coat with sauce. Cover and cook on high for 4 hours. Reduce heat to low and cook another 2 hours. Remove meat to a platter and cover loosely with foil. Let rest 10 minutes. Strain sauce, removing any fat and vegetables that you can. Slice pork and serve with noodles and sauce.

Complete the meal with Sesame Spinach.

Hungarian Pork

8 oz.	wide egg noodles, cooked according to pkg. directions
1 Tbs.	unsalted butter
2 Tbs.	paprika, divided
¼ tsp.	salt
⅛ tsp.	black pepper
1 (1 lb.)	pork tenderloin, cut into 1-inch pieces
2 Tbs.	vegetable oil, divided
1 sm.	yellow onion, finely chopped
1 (14 oz.) can	crushed tomatoes
¼ cup	water
½ cup	sour cream

Stir butter into hot cooked noodles to keep noodles from sticking. Set aside. Combine 1 tablespoon paprika, salt, and pepper and toss with pork pieces. Heat 1 tablespoon oil in a large skillet over medium-high heat. Add pork and cook until lightly browned on all sides, about 4 minutes. Remove pork to a plate and keep warm. In the same skillet, add remaining tablespoon of oil. Reduce heat to medium and cook onions until softened, about 5 minutes. Add pork, remaining tablespoon of paprika, tomatoes, and water. Cook, stirring occasionally, until sauce is slightly thickened, about 3 minutes. Remove from heat. Stir in sour cream. Add more salt or pepper to taste. Serve hot over egg noodles.

Complete the meal with Dilled Lemon Carrots.

Sausage and White Bean Casserole

1 Tbs.	olive oil
6	Italian sausage links, casings removed and crumbled
2	carrots, peeled and cut into bite-size pieces
3	garlic cloves, minced
2 bunches	Swiss chard, cut into strips, or 8 cups fresh baby spinach
2 (15½ oz.) cans	white beans, drained and rinsed
½ cup	water
	salt and pepper to taste
2 Tbs.	bread crumbs
1 tsp.	melted unsalted butter

Preheat oven to 400°F and spray a square baking dish with nonstick cooking spray. Heat oil in a large skillet over medium heat. Add sausage and cook until no longer pink, about 7 minutes. Remove to paper towel to drain. Add carrots and garlic to skillet. Cook, stirring, for 1 minute. Add Swiss chard or spinach leaves to skillet and cook 2 minutes, until wilted. It may seem like too many greens at first, but they will cook down quickly. Add beans, water, salt, and pepper to skillet. Bring to a boil. Remove from heat and carefully stir sausage into mixture. Transfer mixture to baking dish. In a small bowl, mix bread crumbs with melted butter. Sprinkle over casserole. Bake until golden, about 20 minutes.

Complete the meal with Balsamic Roasted Beets or Easy Green Beans.

Tacos al Pastor

1 lb.	pork tenderloin, cut into ½-inch pieces
1 (8 oz.) can	pineapple tidbits in juice, drained
1 med.	red onion, chopped
¼ cup	fresh cilantro, chopped
1 Tbs.	chili powder
1 tsp.	ground cumin
1 tsp.	dried oregano
1 tsp.	pepper
1 tsp.	garlic, chopped
¾ tsp.	salt
1 Tbs.	canola oil
6 (8 in.)	corn or flour tortillas, warmed
	red onion, pineapple, and crumbled white Mexican cheese to garnish, if desired

Combine pork and next 9 ingredients in a large resealable plastic bag. Seal and refrigerate at least 4 hours or up to 24 hours. Heat oil in a large nonstick skillet over medium-high heat. Add pork and marinade and cook for 10 minutes, stirring often. Serve mixture with warm tortillas and desired toppings. Makes 6 tacos.

Complete the meal with Refried Black Beans.

Dijon Baked Pork Chops

2 slices	white bread
½ tsp.	coarse salt
¼ tsp.	pepper
4 (6 oz.)	boneless pork loin chops
1 tsp.	flavored mustard, such as horseradish, wasabi, or roasted garlic

The homemade bread crumbs are important.

Preheat oven to 450°F. In a food processor, pulse bread with coarse salt and pepper until coarse crumbs form. Season pork loin chops on both sides with additional salt and pepper to taste; place on a baking sheet sprayed with cooking spray. Spread top of each chop with mustard. Sprinkle with bread crumbs, patting gently. Bake until golden, about 8–10 minutes, without turning.

Complete the meal with Zucchini and Tomato Bake.

Slow Cooker Garlicky Pork Roast

1 (3 lb.)	boneless pork loin roast
1 Tbs.	vegetable oil
1 tsp.	salt
1 tsp.	coarsely ground black pepper
1 cup	chicken broth
1 med.	yellow onion, sliced
6	garlic cloves, peeled
1½ lbs.	red potatoes, cut in ½-inch-thick slices
1 (16 oz.) bag	baby carrots
½ tsp.	dried thyme

Heat oil in a large skillet over medium-high heat. Brown pork roast in skillet on all sides. Place pork in bottom of slow cooker. Sprinkle with salt and pepper. Add remaining ingredients.

Cover and cook on low for 7–8 hours, until pork and vegetables are tender. Place roast and vegetables on serving platter. Pour juices into a large measuring cup, and skim off as much fat as you can. Serve pork with vegetables and juices.

Complete the meal with Parmesan Tomatoes.

Baked Rigatoni with Ham and Feta Cheese

12 oz.	rigatoni pasta, cooked according to pkg. directions
1½ cups	ham or prosciutto, diced
4 lg.	plum tomatoes, chopped
1 cup	feta cheese, crumbled
1 cup	mozzarella cheese, shredded
1½ tsp.	dried thyme
1 cup	whipping cream
	salt and pepper to taste

Preheat oven to 375°F. Spray a glass 9 x 13 baking dish with nonstick cooking spray. Mix pasta, ham, tomatoes, feta cheese, mozzarella cheese, and thyme in large bowl. Pour cream over. Sprinkle with salt and pepper and toss to blend. Pour mixture into baking dish. Cover with foil and bake 30 minutes. Uncover and bake 15 more minutes. Serves 4–6.

Complete the meal with Winter Pear Salad.

173

MOPS Favorite: Cajun Pork Chops

1 Tbs.	paprika
1 tsp.	seasoned salt
1 tsp.	rubbed sage
½ tsp.	cayenne pepper
½ tsp.	black pepper
½ tsp.	garlic powder
4	boneless pork chops, ½-inch thick
2 Tbs.	unsalted butter

This seasoning is also great on fish fillets.

Combine seasonings. Coat pork chops on both sides with mixture. Heat butter over high heat in a large skillet just until it starts to brown. Watch carefully. Put chops in skillet and reduce heat to medium. Cook both sides until dark brown, about 8–10 minutes total. Do not overcook.

Complete the meal with Bacon Squash Sauté and Quinoa Pilaf with Sun-Dried Tomatoes.

Slow Cooker Cola Ham

½ cup	brown sugar
1 tsp.	dry mustard
¼ cup	cola (I use Coca Cola or Dr Pepper)
1 (3–4 lb.)	precooked ham

Stir together brown sugar and mustard. Moisten with just enough cola to make a smooth paste, and reserve the rest of the cola. Score ham with shallow slashes in a diamond pattern. Rub ham with brown sugar paste and place in slow cooker. Pour remaining cola over. Cover and cook on high for 1 hour. Reduce heat to low and cook for 6 more hours. Serves 8–10.

Complete the meal with Smoked Gouda Macaroni and Cheese and Green Bean Bundles.

Fettuccine with Ham and Peas

5 Tbs.	unsalted butter
1 cup	sliced mushrooms
1 (10 oz.) pkg.	frozen green peas
1–1¼ cups	whipping cream or half-and-half
1 cup	Parmesan cheese, grated
4 oz.	cooked ham or prosciutto, roughly chopped
	salt and pepper to taste
1 lb.	fettuccine, cooked according to pkg. directions

Fat free half-and-half works too, but it will make a thinner sauce.

Melt butter in a large skillet over medium heat. Add mushrooms and sauté for 3 minutes. Add green peas and stir to heat through, about 30 seconds. Add cream and bring to a low boil. Boil for 2 minutes, stirring constantly. Reduce heat and stir in Parmesan cheese and ham. Season with salt and pepper as desired. Place fettuccine in a large serving bowl. Top with pasta sauce and mix well to combine. Serve immediately.

Barbecue Pork Chops

8 (8 oz.)	boneless pork loin chops, ¾-inch thick
2 Tbs.	canola oil
½ cup	brown sugar, packed
½ cup	sweet onion, chopped
½ cup	ketchup
½ cup	barbecue sauce
½ cup	French salad dressing
½ cup	honey

In a large skillet, working in batches, brown pork chops in oil on both sides, being careful not to overcook. Return all pork chops to skillet. Combine remaining ingredients; pour over chops. Bring to a boil. Reduce heat. Cover and simmer for 12–14 minutes or until a meat thermometer reads 160°F. Serve immediately, or cool before freezing. Freeze up to 3 months. Serves 8.

Complete the meal with Smoked Gouda Macaroni and Cheese.

Busy Day Pork Chops

4	thick center-cut pork chops
1 cup	ketchup
1 Tbs.	garlic chili sauce, optional
¼ cup	water
¼ cup	Worcestershire sauce
¾ cup	brown sugar
¼ cup	lemon juice

Preheat oven to 250°F. Combine all ingredients except pork chops. Place pork chops in a 2-quart glass baking dish. Pour sauce over chops. Bake, uncovered, 2½–3 hours.

Complete the meal with rice and Homemade Applesauce.

Thai Pork Curry

1 (1 lb.)	pork tenderloin
1 Tbs. + 1–2 tsp.	mild curry powder
2 Tbs.	canola oil, divided
⅔ cup	canned unsweetened coconut milk
1 cup	vegetable or chicken broth
2 Tbs.	fresh basil, chopped
16 oz.	frozen green beans, prepared according to pkg. directions

Preheat oven to 350°F. Mix 1 tablespoon curry powder with 1 tablespoon of oil to create a paste. Rub tenderloin all over with paste. Heat remaining tablespoon of oil in an ovenproof skillet over high heat. Add pork and brown on all sides, about 4 minutes. Transfer skillet to oven. Bake about 15 minutes, until internal meat thermometer reads 155°F. Remove from oven and let pork rest 5 minutes.

In a saucepan over medium-low heat, blend remaining curry powder (1–2 teaspoons or more, to taste) and a dash of coconut milk until smooth. Add remaining milk and vegetable broth. Simmer about 5 minutes. Remove from heat and stir in basil. Slice pork thinly and place on serving platter, with green beans around the edges. Pour warm sauce over pork. Serve with rice.

Slow-Cooker Cuban Pork

¼ cup	lime juice
¼ cup	grapefruit juice
¼ cup	water
3	garlic cloves, minced
1 tsp.	dried oregano
½ tsp.	ground cumin
½ tsp.	salt
¼ tsp.	pepper
4 lbs.	boneless pork shoulder
1 cup	white onion, sliced
	flour tortillas

Mix together all ingredients except pork, onion, and tortillas. Pierce pork shoulder several times with a fork. Place pork in a large resealable plastic bag, and pour marinade over. Refrigerate at least 6 hours and up to 24 hours, turning occasionally. Lay onion slices in bottom of slow cooker. Top with meat. Pour marinade over. Cook on low for 10–12 hours, until tender. Remove meat and shred with 2 forks. Pour gravy from slow cooker into a large measuring cup. Remove as much fat as you can from the surface. Strain gravy into a large bowl and serve with meat and flour tortillas. Serves 8.

Complete the meal with Fresh Summer Corn Salad.

Lamb Tandoori

2 lbs.	boneless leg of lamb
1 cup	plain yogurt
2 Tbs.	canola oil
1 Tbs.	garlic, finely chopped
2 tsp.	fresh ginger, finely chopped
1 tsp.	ground coriander
1 tsp.	ground cumin
½–1 tsp.	cayenne pepper
¼ tsp.	ground cinnamon
1 tsp.	ground turmeric
2 tsp.	paprika
½ tsp.	salt

Put all ingredients except lamb in large bowl and whisk to combine. Add lamb. Turn to coat with yogurt marinade. Cover and refrigerate for 2–4 hours, turning occasionally. Preheat grill to medium-high heat. Remove meat from refrigerator and discard marinade. Grill lamb, turning once, until desired doneness (about 140°F for medium). Serve warm. Serves 4–6.

Complete the meal with Herbed Lentils.

Herbed Lamb Chops

2 lg.	garlic cloves, minced
1 Tbs.	fresh rosemary
1 tsp.	fresh thyme
⅛ tsp.	cayenne pepper
	salt to taste
2 Tbs.	olive oil
6	lamb chops, ¾-inch thick

Process garlic, rosemary, thyme, cayenne, and salt in a food processor. Slowly add olive oil and process until a paste forms. Rub paste on both sides of lamb chops. Refrigerate, covered, for 1 hour. Remove lamb chops 20 minutes before cooking. Heat a large skillet over high heat. When very hot, add chops and cook for about 2 minutes. Flip and cook for another 3½ minutes. Remove from heat. Serve immediately. Serves 6.

Complete the meal with Curried Rice Salad.

Almond Baked Fish

2 tsp.	lemon juice
¼ tsp.	salt
3 Tbs. + 2 tsp.	unsalted butter, melted
4 (¼ lb.)	flounder or other white fish fillets
⅓ cup	mayonnaise
½ cup	cracker crumbs, any kind
2 Tbs.	slivered almonds

Heat oven to 400°F. Combine lemon juice, salt, and 2 teaspoons butter in a 9 x 13 casserole dish. Arrange fish in dish. Spread mayonnaise over fish. Combine cracker crumbs, remaining 3 tablespoons melted butter, and almonds. Sprinkle over fish. Bake for 10–15 minutes, until fish is white all the way through.

Complete the meal with Glazed Brussels Sprouts with Bacon and Parmesan Tomatoes.

Grilled Shrimp

2 lbs.	large, fresh shrimp, peeled and deveined
4	garlic cloves, minced
1 cup	vegetable oil
½ cup	fresh basil, chopped
2 Tbs.	white vinegar
1 Tbs.	Worcestershire sauce
½ tsp.	hot pepper sauce
6 (12 in.)	skewers

Combine all ingredients except shrimp in a medium bowl. Mix well. Add shrimp and toss gently to coat. Cover and marinate at least 30 minutes and up to 4 hours, stirring occasionally. Remove shrimp from marinade. Place shrimp on skewers. Grill over medium-hot heat for 3–4 minutes on each side, until shrimp is pink.

Complete the meal with Garlic Cheese Grits.

Pesto Fish Kabobs

1½ lbs.	halibut, cod, or red snapper, cut into 1-inch pieces
1 lg.	red bell pepper, cut into 1-inch pieces
3 Tbs.	basil pesto
2 Tbs.	white vinegar
½ tsp.	salt
4 (12 in.)	skewers

Preheat oven broiler. Place fish and bell pepper in a shallow glass dish. Combine pesto and vinegar and drizzle over fish and peppers. Toss to coat. Let stand 5 minutes. Thread fish and peppers alternately onto skewers, then place on a jellyroll pan coated with nonstick cooking spray. Broil 8 minutes or until fish is cooked through, turning once.

Complete the meal with Zucchini Fries.

Spaghetti with Shrimp and Bacon

12 oz.	spaghetti, cooked according to pkg. directions
1 cup	water, reserved from cooking pasta
2	bacon slices, chopped
8 oz.	large frozen shrimp, peeled and deveined, thawed and halved horizontally
6	green onions, chopped
2	garlic cloves, minced
1 Tbs.	fresh lemon juice
	salt and black pepper to taste

While pasta is cooking, fry bacon in a large skillet over medium heat until browned, 6–8 minutes. Drain on paper towel. Add shrimp, green onions, and garlic to same skillet. Cook, stirring frequently, until shrimp are almost opaque, about 1 minute. Add reserved pasta water, and bring just to a boil. Combine shrimp mixture and lemon juice with cooked pasta. Season with salt and pepper, and toss to combine. Serve sprinkled with bacon.

Complete the meal with Italian Caprese Salad.

Linguine with Shrimp and Sun-Dried Tomatoes

16 oz.	linguine
1 (7 oz.) jar	sun-dried tomatoes in oil
¼ cup	pine nuts
¼ cup	extra virgin olive oil
3	garlic cloves, minced
16 med.	cooked shrimp
4 oz.	feta cheese, crumbled
2 Tbs.	fresh basil, thinly sliced

Prepare linguine according to package directions. Drain tomatoes, reserving 2 tablespoons of the oil, and slice thinly. Heat a dry skillet over medium-low heat and add pine nuts. Cook, stirring, until toasted, about 5 minutes. Remove pine nuts from skillet. Add the reserved sun-dried tomato oil plus olive oil to the skillet and increase heat to medium. Add garlic and shrimp and sauté just until heated through, about 1 minute. Stir in tomatoes. Remove from heat and toss with linguine, feta, and basil. Top with toasted pine nuts. Good hot or cold.

Complete the meal with Easy Greek Salad.

Shrimp with Smoked Paprika-Tomato Sauce

1 lb.	large fresh shrimp (can use frozen and thawed)
½ tsp.	granulated garlic
1 tsp.	smoked paprika, divided
½ tsp.	salt
pinch	cayenne pepper
2 Tbs.	olive oil
4	garlic cloves, coarsely chopped
1 (14.5 oz.) can	diced tomatoes, undrained
	freshly ground black pepper

Peel and devein the shrimp and pat dry. Mix granulated garlic, ½ teaspoon of smoked paprika, salt, and cayenne pepper. Sprinkle over shrimp. Allow to sit for at least 5 minutes. Heat olive oil in a medium skillet over medium-high heat. Add garlic and cook until golden brown and fragrant. Add shrimp and sear for 2 minutes. Add diced tomatoes, ground black pepper, and remaining smoked paprika. Reduce heat to medium and cook for 4 more minutes or until shrimp are no longer translucent.

Complete the meal: serve over buttered fettuccine with Roasted Balsamic Asparagus.

Curried Shrimp

2 Tbs.	olive oil
2 sm.	yellow onions, chopped
2 Tbs.	fresh ginger, peeled and minced
2 Tbs.	curry powder
2 (14 oz.) cans	unsweetened coconut milk
16 lg.	fresh shrimp, peeled and deveined
¼ cup	fresh cilantro, chopped
	salt and pepper to taste

Unsweetened coconut milk can be found at most supermarkets in the Asian and Indian cooking aisle.

Heat oil in large skillet over medium-high heat. Add onion and sauté until soft, about 3–4 minutes. Add ginger and curry powder, and sauté 1 minute. Stir in coconut milk and simmer 6 minutes. Add shrimp and simmer until shrimp is opaque in center, about 3–4 minutes. Stir in cilantro. Season with salt and pepper to taste.

Complete the meal with rice and Broccoli and Green Bean Duo.

Salmon with Buttery Almonds

4 Tbs.	unsalted butter, divided
1½ lbs.	skinless salmon fillet, quartered
	salt and black pepper to taste
¼ cup	slivered almonds
2 Tbs.	capers

Heat 1 tablespoon butter in a large nonstick skillet over medium heat. Season salmon with salt and pepper. Place salmon in skillet and cook 5 minutes per side, until salmon is opaque. Transfer to platter to keep warm. In same skillet, melt remaining butter over medium-high heat. Add almonds and cook, stirring frequently, until butter and almonds turn a golden brown, about 3 minutes. Stir in capers. Spoon over salmon and serve immediately.

Complete the meal: serve with a simple orzo pasta and Garlic Citrus Spinach.

Ginger-Glazed Halibut

2 Tbs.	light brown sugar
1 Tbs.	soy sauce
2 tsp.	fresh ginger, minced
1	garlic clove, minced
4 (6 oz.)	halibut or cod fillets
2 Tbs.	canola oil
	salt and black pepper to taste

Preheat oven broiler, and line a baking sheet with foil. In a small bowl, combine brown sugar, soy sauce, ginger, and garlic. Place fish on baking sheet. Brush with oil and season with salt and pepper. Broil 4 minutes. Baste fish with soy sauce mixture and return to oven for 1 minute. Repeat basting 2 more times. Fish should be opaque throughout. Serve immediately.

Complete the meal with Sesame Spinach.

Sesame Scallops

16 lg.	sea scallops
1	green onion, sliced and divided by color
2	garlic cloves, minced
2 Tbs.	soy sauce
1 Tbs.	rice vinegar
1 Tbs.	sugar
½ tsp.	cornstarch
1 Tbs.	sesame oil
⅛ tsp.	crushed red pepper flakes
1 tsp.	canola oil
⅛ tsp.	black pepper

Take scallops out of refrigerator while you prepare recipe. Combine white parts of onion with garlic, soy sauce, rice vinegar, sugar, cornstarch, sesame oil, and crushed red pepper flakes. Set aside.

Heat canola oil in a large nonstick skillet over medium heat. Add scallops. Sprinkle top side with black pepper. Cook 3 minutes, until golden brown on bottom. Flip and cook 3 more minutes. Remove scallops to a platter and keep warm. In same skillet, add sauce mixture and cook until boiling, about 30 seconds. Remove from heat. Pour sauce over scallops, garnish with green onion, and serve immediately.

Complete the meal with Thai Noodle Salad.

Artichoke Spinach Lasagna

9	lasagna noodles, uncooked
1	yellow onion, chopped
3	garlic cloves, chopped
1 (14.5 oz.) can	vegetable broth
1 (14 oz.) can	marinated artichoke hearts, drained and chopped
1 (10 oz.) pkg.	frozen chopped spinach, thawed, drained, and squeezed dry
1 (28 oz.) jar	marinara sauce
3 cups	mozzarella cheese, shredded and divided
4 oz.	feta cheese, crumbled

Preheat oven to 350°F. Spray a 9 x 13 baking dish with cooking spray. Fill a large pot with lightly salted water and bring to a boil. Add lasagna noodles and cook 8–10 minutes until done but not soggy. Drain water. Spray large skillet with cooking spray and heat over medium heat. Sauté onion and garlic 3 minutes. Stir in broth. Bring to a boil and add artichoke hearts and spinach. Reduce heat and simmer 5 minutes. Add pasta sauce and stir. Spread a quarter of artichoke and pasta sauce mixture in bottom of baking dish. Top with 3 cooked noodles. Sprinkle 1 cup mozzarella cheese over. Repeat layers twice, ending with artichoke mixture and mozzarella. Top with crumbled feta cheese. Cover with aluminum foil and bake 40 minutes. Uncover and bake 15 more minutes until bubbly. Let stand at least 10 minutes before cutting.

Complete the meal with Italian Salad.

Vegetarian Noodles with Lime Peanut Sauce

½ cup	crunchy peanut butter or soy butter
¼ cup	soy sauce
¼ cup	hot water
2 Tbs.	rice vinegar
2 Tbs.	lime juice
1	green onion, chopped
2 Tbs.	fresh ginger, grated
2 Tbs.	brown sugar
¼ tsp.	red pepper flakes
1 lb.	linguine, cooked according to pkg. directions
1 lb.	broccoli florets, steamed
2 cups	sugar snap peas, steamed

Purée peanut butter, soy sauce, hot water, rice vinegar, lime juice, green onion, ginger, brown sugar, and red pepper flakes in a food processor. Toss with pasta and steamed vegetables. Garnish with additional peanuts if desired. Serves 4–6.

Farmer's Market Stir-Fry

2 cups	eggplant, peeled and diced
1 tsp.	salt
2½ Tbs.	canola oil, divided
2½ Tbs.	red wine vinegar
1 cup	carrots, peeled and diced
1 cup	zucchini, diced
1 cup	yellow squash, diced
1 cup	small broccoli florets
1 cup	red bell pepper, diced
½ cup	onion, diced
2	garlic cloves, minced
1 cup	couscous, prepared according to pkg. directions
¼ cup	fresh basil, chopped
	salt and pepper to taste
2 Tbs.	toasted pine nuts, optional

Toss eggplant and salt in medium bowl. Let stand 30 minutes. Rinse and drain. Pat dry. Whisk 1½ tablespoons oil with vinegar in small bowl. Heat remaining 1 tablespoon oil in wok or large nonstick skillet over medium-high heat. Add eggplant and carrots. Stir-fry 3 minutes. Add zucchini and next 5 ingredients. Stir-fry until vegetables are crisp-tender, about 2 minutes. Add couscous and vinegar mixture. Stir-fry 1 minute. Stir in basil. Season to taste with salt and pepper. Sprinkle with pine nuts, if desired.

Pasta Primavera

12 oz.	linguine or spaghetti, cooked according to pkg. directions
1 Tbs.	olive oil
3	garlic cloves, minced
1½ cups	small broccoli florets
1½ cups	zucchini, diced
1 cup	carrots, thinly sliced
1	sweet red pepper, cut in thin strips
¼ cup	white cooking wine
1 tsp.	dried thyme
½ cup	Parmesan cheese, grated
¼ tsp.	black pepper

Heat oil in a large nonstick skillet over medium-high heat. Add garlic and stir-fry for 30 seconds. Add broccoli, zucchini, carrots, and red pepper. Stir-fry for 4 minutes. Add cooking wine and cook 1 minute. Transfer vegetables to large bowl and sprinkle with thyme. Add hot pasta. Sprinkle with Parmesan cheese and pepper. Toss and serve hot.

Vegetarian White Beans with Kale and Rigatoni

1 cup	yellow onion, chopped
2	garlic cloves, minced
2 Tbs.	olive oil
8 oz.	fresh mushrooms, sliced
2 (15 oz.) cans	cannellini beans, rinsed and drained
2 (14.5 oz.) cans	diced tomatoes, undrained
1 tsp.	salt
½ tsp.	pepper
3 cups	kale, chopped
16 oz.	rigatoni pasta, cooked according to pkg. directions
½ cup	Parmesan cheese, shredded

In a large saucepan, sauté onion and garlic in oil until tender. Stir in mushrooms and cook 5 minutes over medium heat. Stir in beans, tomatoes, salt, and pepper. Bring to a boil. Reduce heat and simmer, uncovered, for 5 minutes. Stir in kale. Cover and cook for 3–4 minutes or until kale is wilted. Add pasta to bean mixture and heat through. Sprinkle with Parmesan cheese. Serve warm.

Vegetarian Eggplant Parmesan

1 lg.	eggplant, peeled and cut into ¼-inch-thick slices
2	eggs
1 Tbs.	water
1 cup	bread crumbs
⅔ cup + 2 Tbs.	olive oil, divided
	salt to taste
6 oz.	mushrooms, sliced
1 (26 oz.) jar	marinara sauce
15 oz.	ricotta cheese
2 cups	mozzarella cheese, thinly sliced
1½ cups	Parmesan cheese, grated

Preheat oven to 400°F. Spray a baking sheet and a 9 x 13 casserole dish with nonstick cooking spray. Beat eggs with water in a small bowl. Dip eggplant slices in egg wash, then in plate of bread crumbs. Layer eggplant on baking sheet, slightly overlapping. Drizzle with ⅓ cup olive oil and sprinkle with salt. Bake 20 minutes. Remove from oven and turn. Drizzle with another ⅓ cup olive oil and salt to taste. Bake 20 more minutes. Set aside. While eggplant is cooking, sauté mushrooms in remaining 2 tablespoons olive oil in large skillet over medium heat about 4 minutes. Remove from heat and add marinara sauce. Mix well.

Reduce oven temperature to 350°F. Cover bottom of casserole dish with half of the sauce. Add half the eggplant slices, spreading in an even layer. Spoon half of the ricotta over, and top with half of the mozzarella and Parmesan. Repeat layers. Bake approximately 45 minutes or until bubbly. Serves 6.

Complete the meal with Herbed Spaghetti Squash.

Vegetarian Spinach and Ricotta Shells

16	jumbo pasta shells, cooked according to pkg. directions
2 tsp.	olive oil
1 cup	frozen chopped spinach, thawed and squeezed dry
2	garlic cloves, minced
8 oz.	ricotta cheese
8 oz.	mozzarella cheese, shredded
1	egg, lightly beaten
1 Tbs.	fresh basil, chopped
2 cups	marinara sauce
2 Tbs.	Parmesan cheese, grated

Toss cooked pasta shells with oil in a large bowl. Set aside. Preheat oven to 375°F. In a large bowl, combine spinach, garlic, ricotta, mozzarella, egg, and basil. Mix well.

Spread ½ cup of the marinara sauce in the bottom of a 9 x 13 baking dish that has been sprayed with nonstick cooking spray. Fill each pasta shell with spinach mixture and arrange in the dish. Pour remaining sauce over and around the stuffed shells and top with Parmesan. Cover with foil and bake 25 minutes. Uncover and continue baking 10 more minutes.

Vegetarian Layered Enchiladas

2 cups	frozen corn, thawed
1 cup	bell pepper strips
3 Tbs.	lime juice, divided
2 Tbs.	chili powder, divided
1 (15 oz.) can	diced tomatoes with green chiles
8 oz.	frozen chopped spinach, thawed and squeezed dry
1 (15 oz.) can	black beans, rinsed and drained
4 Tbs.	cilantro, chopped and divided
8 (6 in.)	corn tortillas
¾ cup	mozzarella cheese, shredded, optional
	sour cream and salsa to garnish as desired

Preheat oven to 400°F and spray a 9 x 13 casserole dish with nonstick cooking spray. In a large pot, combine corn, bell peppers, 2 tablespoons lime juice, 1 tablespoon chili powder, tomatoes, and spinach, and cook over medium-high heat for 10 minutes. Mash black beans with 2 tablespoons cilantro, 1 tablespoon chili powder, and 1 tablespoon lime juice.

Place four tortillas in bottom of casserole, overlapping a bit. Spread bean mixture evenly over each. Spread half of the vegetable mixture and a sprinkling of cheese, if using. Top with remaining tortillas, vegetables, and cheese, if using, and bake until heated through and cheese is melted, about 15 minutes. Transfer to plates and garnish with remaining cilantro, sour cream, and salsa, if desired. Serves 4–6.

Sweet and Sour Tofu

1 lb.	firm tofu, cut into bite-size cubes
1 cup	prepared soy ginger stir-fry sauce, divided
1 Tbs.	canola oil
1	red bell pepper, seeded and chopped
1	green bell pepper, seeded and chopped
½ cup	yellow onion, chopped
2 cups	pineapple, cut into ¾-inch chunks
1 Tbs.	rice vinegar
2	green onions, thinly sliced
	chopped, roasted peanuts to garnish, if desired

Gently toss tofu cubes in ¼ cup of the soy ginger sauce. Heat canola oil in a wok or large nonstick skillet over medium-high heat. Add tofu and cook, stirring occasionally, until golden brown. Transfer tofu to a large plate and keep warm. Add bell peppers and onions to skillet and cook, stirring occasionally, for 3 minutes. Add pineapple and cook 3 minutes more. Reduce heat to medium-low. Add remaining ¾ cup soy ginger sauce, vinegar, and green onions and stir gently once or twice. Gently stir in tofu and heat through. To serve, top with peanuts, if desired.

Complete the meal with rice or noodles and Crunchy Asian Slaw.

Vegetarian Stuffed Peppers

4	poblano peppers, cut in half lengthwise and seeded
1¼ cups	fresh or frozen corn kernels, thawed
1 (15 oz.) can	black beans, drained and rinsed
¾ cup	brown rice, cooked according to pkg. directions
3 Tbs.	olive oil
1 tsp.	salt
¼ tsp.	black pepper
4 oz.	feta or goat cheese, crumbled

Preheat oven broiler. Adjust rack to the highest position. Place poblanos skin side up on a foil-lined baking sheet. Broil until skin is charred, about 3 minutes. Remove from oven and let cool.

In a large bowl, combine corn, beans, cooked rice, oil, salt, and pepper. Remove skin from poblanos (it's easiest to use your fingers) and discard. Spoon rice mixture into the peppers and sprinkle with cheese. Serve at room temperature.

Complete the meal with Summer Tomato Cheese Tart.

CHAPTER 8

Side Dishes

That's something I've noticed about food: whenever there's a crisis if you can get people to eating normally things get better.

Madeleine L'Engle

Thanksgiving at my house is all about the side dishes. We know we're going to have smoked turkey, but the real excitement comes with the countless sensational side dishes that fill up our holiday bellies.

And if you're like me, you're quite particular about those side dishes. At my house, our sweet potatoes don't have marshmallows, and our corn bread dressing (not stuffing) has to be my grandmother's recipe. Show up with something else, and we might escort you straight out the back door.

I'm just kidding, but a co-worker told me one year that the only way he was going to have a good Thanksgiving dinner was if he could eat alone.

Unfortunately, family dinners can turn into nightmares in a matter of seconds. Uncle Billy announces at the table that your mashed potatoes taste like wallpaper paste. Aunt Marjorie asks you (again) why you're not having more children. And your tipsy father reminds you about the time (when you were seven) that you said you were going to move back home to join him in the family business when you grew up.

And not every criticism is that obvious. Silence among family members can hurt far worse, and suddenly you find yourself eating and leaving as fast as you can.

We all have family members whom we wouldn't choose to spend time with on a daily basis, even for just a few hours. But the days of my family all being together are numbered, as are yours, and I want to try and find the good in every crazy person in our family tree.

The biblical story of the Prodigal Son is about a family and a feast. The younger, wayward brother returns home to a place of forgiveness and feasting. The older, obedient brother refuses to enjoy the homecoming. He stays outside, feasting only on past wrongs and self-righteous misbehavior. I bet he was hungry though.

Your family is connected to you in some way, whether you chose them or not. And there is something to learn from each of them, and something you can give back. Life is so much easier when we decide to see the good in each other, and to feast on the love gathered around the family table.

O Lord, we thank Thee for our daily bread. May it strengthen and refresh our bodies! And we pray Thee, nourish our souls with Thy heavenly grace, through Jesus Christ, our Lord. Amen.

Chili-Roasted Sweet Potatoes

4 cups	sweet potatoes, peeled and cubed (approx. 4 med.)
2 tsp.	ground cumin
1 tsp.	chili powder
½ tsp.	smoked paprika
½ tsp.	salt
¼ tsp.	cayenne pepper
1½ Tbs.	olive oil

Preheat oven to 425°F. Put potatoes in a mixing bowl and add dry seasonings. Toss to coat evenly. Drizzle with olive oil and toss again. Arrange potatoes in a single layer in a shallow baking pan lined with foil. Roast on the lower rack for 8 minutes. Turn potatoes and continue roasting until tender, 6–10 more minutes. Serve warm. Serves 4.

Baked Sweet Potato Sticks

1 Tbs.	olive oil
½ tsp.	paprika
8	sweet potatoes, peeled and sliced lengthwise into quarters

Preheat oven to 400°F. Lightly spray a baking sheet with nonstick cooking spray. In a large mixing bowl, combine olive oil and paprika. Add quartered potatoes and stir well to coat evenly. Place on baking sheet in a single layer. Bake for 40 minutes. Remove from oven and serve warm or at room temperature. Serves 8.

Thanksgiving Sweet Potatoes

3 cups	sweet potatoes, cooked and mashed
2	eggs, beaten
1 cup	sugar
½ cup	unsalted butter, melted
1 tsp.	vanilla extract
pinch	salt

You can omit the pecans if your family doesn't eat nuts.

For topping:

½ cup	chopped pecans
1 cup	brown sugar
⅓ cup	all-purpose flour
½ cup	unsalted butter, softened

Preheat oven to 350°F. Spray a 9 x 13 casserole dish with nonstick cooking spray. Mix sweet potatoes with eggs, sugar, melted butter, vanilla, and salt. Mix thoroughly and pour in dish. For the topping, combine pecans, sugar, flour, and softened butter to make a crumbly streusel. Sprinkle over potatoes. Bake 30–40 minutes.

Bacon Squash Sauté

6	bacon slices, diced
4 sm.	yellow summer squash, sliced ¼-inch thick
1 med.	sweet onion, thinly sliced

In a large skillet, cook bacon over medium heat until crisp; remove to paper towel. Drain, reserving 2 tablespoons drippings. In the drippings, sauté the squash and onion for 6–8 minutes or until crisp-tender. Sprinkle with crumbled bacon.

Herbed Spaghetti Squash

1 (2–2½ lb.)	spaghetti squash
3 Tbs.	unsalted butter or olive oil
1 Tbs.	basil, chopped
1 Tbs.	chives, chopped
1 Tbs.	parsley, chopped
	salt and pepper to taste

Also great with ¼ cup grated Parmesan cheese sprinkled over.

Preheat the oven to 375°F. Using a sharp knife, cut squash in half lengthwise and place, cut sides down, in a 9 x 13 baking dish. Add enough water to come half an inch up the sides of the baking dish, and cover with aluminum foil. Bake for 45 minutes, until the squash is easily pierced with a paring knife. Turn squash over, re-cover with foil, and continue to cook another 15 minutes, until the squash is very tender. Allow squash to cool slightly. Remove the seeds with a spoon and discard. Using a fork, gently pull the strands of squash away from the rind and place the squash strands into a mixing bowl. Heat a large skillet over medium-high heat. Add butter or olive oil, spaghetti squash, herbs, salt, and pepper and toss thoroughly but gently to combine. Heat through. Serve immediately or cover and keep warm until ready to serve. Serves 6.

Maple Roasted Butternut Squash

2 med.	butternut squash, halved lengthwise and seeded
½ cup	unsalted butter
⅓ cup	maple syrup
¼ tsp.	cinnamon

Preheat oven to 400°F. Score cut sides of butternut squash diagonally in 2 directions and place cut sides up in a 9 x 13 baking dish. Melt butter in saucepan over medium heat. Add maple syrup and cinnamon. Stir until blended. Brush butter mixture over squash. Add enough water to come half an inch up sides of baking dish. Bake 50–60 minutes, until squash is tender. Serves 4–6.

Squash Casserole

2 lbs.	yellow summer squash, sliced ¼-inch thick
1 cup	onion, chopped
1 tsp.	salt
¼ tsp.	black pepper
	water
¼ cup	unsalted butter
1 cup	saltine crackers, crumbled
½ cup	milk
1 cup	cheddar cheese, shredded
½ cup	bread crumbs

Preheat oven to 350°F. Place squash, onion, salt, and pepper in a large saucepan. Add enough water to cover bottom of pan. Cover and cook squash until tender, stirring occasionally and adding more water if necessary. Drain. Return vegetables to pan and stir in butter. Taste and adjust seasonings, adding more salt and pepper, if desired. Spray a 1½-quart casserole dish with nonstick cooking spray. Stir crumbled crackers into the squash mixture, and scoop into the casserole dish. Pour milk over squash and sprinkle with cheese and bread crumbs. Bake, uncovered, for 20 minutes, until bubbly. Serve hot. Serves 4–6.

MOPS Favorite: Zucchini and Tomato Bake

4 sm.	zucchini, thinly sliced
4 sm.	tomatoes, diced
1 sm.	yellow onion, thinly sliced
	salt and pepper to taste
2 Tbs.	brown sugar
2 tsp.	Italian seasoning
¾ cup	bread crumbs
1 cup	cheddar cheese, grated
¼ cup	unsalted butter, melted

Preheat oven to 350°F. Spray a deep 2-quart casserole dish with nonstick cooking spray. Layer half of the zucchini, tomatoes, and onions in the dish. Sprinkle with half of the brown sugar and Italian seasoning, then salt and pepper to taste. Sprinkle with half of the bread crumbs and cheese. Drizzle with half of the butter. Repeat layers. Bake covered for 30 minutes. Uncover and continue baking for 5 minutes, until center is bubbling. Serves 6.

Zucchini Fries

1½ cups	panko (Japanese bread crumbs)
¾ cup	Parmesan cheese, shredded
1½ tsp.	Italian seasoning
¼ tsp.	cayenne pepper
¾ tsp.	salt
¼ tsp.	black pepper
2 lg.	egg whites, lightly beaten
2 lg.	zucchini, halved and cut into bite-size sticks

Serve with buttermilk ranch dressing for dipping.

Preheat oven to 425°F. Spray 2 baking sheets with nonstick cooking spray. In a shallow dish, combine panko, Parmesan cheese, Italian seasoning, cayenne pepper, salt, and black pepper. Dip zucchini sticks in egg whites and then bread crumbs, pressing to coat zucchini well. Place on baking sheets. Bake on separate oven racks for 20 minutes or until crisp, turning zucchini halfway through and rotating baking sheet positions. Season fries with salt and pepper as desired. Serve hot.

Grilled Street Corn

4 ears	sweet corn, husks removed
2 Tbs.	corn oil
½ cup	mayonnaise
1 tsp.	chili powder
1 tsp.	garlic salt
	black pepper to taste

Preheat grill to medium-high heat. Rub corn with oil and grill, turning frequently so all sides are evenly charred, about 6–10 minutes. Meanwhile, mix together mayonnaise, chili powder, garlic salt, and black pepper. Remove corn from grill and brush with mayonnaise mixture.

Southwest Creamed Corn

3 Tbs.	unsalted butter
1 sm.	yellow onion, diced
1 med.	sweet red pepper, diced
1	jalapeño pepper, diced
2 lg.	garlic cloves, minced
3 cups	fresh corn kernels, with juice
1 tsp.	ground cumin
1 tsp.	smoked paprika
¼ cup	heavy cream
2 oz.	cream cheese
	salt and black pepper

Melt the butter in a large sauté pan. Add onion, sweet pepper, and jalapeño pepper. Cover the pan and sweat the veggies over medium-low heat for about 5–7 minutes. "Sweating" means we are not looking to add any color, but just simmering the mixture in a covered pan. Add garlic and cook 1 minute. Add corn kernels and any juice. Cook over low heat for a few minutes, then add cumin, paprika, cream, cream cheese, and salt and pepper to taste. Mix well but gently, so as not to squash the corn too much; cover the pan and simmer for about 6–8 minutes. Taste and adjust seasonings as desired.

Lightened Creamed Corn

¼ cup	butter substitute, such as Smart Balance Buttery Sticks
4 cups	fresh corn kernels
½ tsp.	salt
1 Tbs.	all-purpose flour
¾ cup	fat free half-and-half
	black pepper to taste

Heat butter substitute in a large skillet over medium heat. Add corn kernels and salt. Stir well to coat. Cook 5 minutes, stirring occasionally. Don't let the corn brown. Sprinkle flour over and stir well. Cook 2 minutes. Add half-and-half, stirring well. Simmer 3–4 more minutes until corn is tender and half-and-half starts to thicken. If corn is starchy, you may need to add a bit more half-and-half. Add salt and pepper to taste. Serve immediately. Serves 4–6.

Oven-Roasted Green Beans

1½ lbs.	fresh green beans, trimmed
2 Tbs.	extra virgin olive oil
1 tsp.	kosher salt
½ tsp.	freshly ground black pepper

Preheat oven to 425°F. Toss beans with olive oil, salt, and pepper, and spread out evenly on a parchment-lined baking sheet. Roast, stirring once halfway through, until lightly caramelized and crisp-tender, 12–15 minutes. Serves 6.

Updated Green Bean Casserole

4 Tbs.	unsalted butter, divided
2 Tbs.	all-purpose flour
1 Tbs.	sugar
¼ tsp.	pepper
½ tsp.	salt
1 Tbs.	onion, chopped
1 cup	sour cream
2 (14.5 oz.) cans	whole green beans, drained
½ lb.	Swiss cheese, shredded
1 cup	bread crumbs

Preheat oven to 350°F. Melt 2 tablespoons of butter in a large saucepan over medium-low heat. Add flour, sugar, pepper, salt, and onion.

Stir in sour cream and heat through, but do not boil. Stir in green beans and cheese, and pour into greased casserole dish. Melt remaining butter and toss with bread crumbs; sprinkle on casserole. Bake uncovered for 20 minutes. Serves 6.

Easy Green Beans

1 lb.	fresh green beans
½ cup	bread crumbs
½ tsp.	garlic salt
¼ cup	Parmesan cheese
1–2 Tbs.	olive oil

Fill a large pot with water and bring to a boil over high heat. While waiting for water to boil, wash green beans and trim ends if necessary. Once water is boiling, toss green beans in pot and boil about 4 minutes, until bright green. While beans are boiling, mix together the dry ingredients in a separate bowl. Drain beans and toss with olive oil. Sprinkle crumb mixture over the beans and serve immediately. Serves 6.

Green Bean Bundles

3 (14.5 oz.) cans	whole green beans, drained
2 cups	reduced fat French salad dressing
12–16	bacon slices, halved

Gently toss green beans with French dressing. Cover and refrigerate at least 1 hour or up to overnight. When ready to bake, preheat oven to 350°F. Spray a 9 x 13 casserole dish with nonstick cooking spray. Divide beans equally among bacon slice halves to make bundles. Wrap bacon slices around beans and lay bundles, seam side down, in bottom of casserole dish. Bake for 20–25 minutes, until bacon is browned. Serves 6–8.

Cranberry Wild Rice Pilaf

2½ cups	chicken broth
1 cup	basmati and wild rice mix
½ cup	green onions, chopped
½ cup	pecan pieces, toasted
½ cup	dried cranberries

Bring chicken broth to a boil in a medium saucepan. Add rice mix and return to boil. Stir once, and cover. Simmer over low heat until rice is tender and broth is absorbed, about 30 minutes. Remove from heat. Just before serving, toss rice with green onions, pecans, and cranberries. Can be served warm or at room temperature.

Brown Rice Risotto

2½ cups	chicken stock
1 Tbs.	unsalted butter
1 cup	long-grain brown rice
1 cup	Parmesan cheese, grated

Bring chicken stock to a boil. Add butter. When butter is melted, stir in rice. Reduce heat to a simmer. Cover and cook 45 minutes. Remove from heat and fluff with a fork. Stir in cheese and serve immediately.

Artichoke Rice

1 pkg.	chicken-flavored rice, such as Uncle Ben's
2 (6 oz.) jars	marinated artichoke hearts, liquid reserved
⅓ cup	mayonnaise
¾ tsp.	curry powder
4	green onions, sliced
½	bell pepper, seeded and chopped
12	green olives, halved

Cook rice according to package directions. Mix liquid from artichoke hearts, mayonnaise, and curry powder. Add this mixture to onions, bell pepper, olives, and artichoke hearts. Gradually add rice, stirring carefully. Serve warm or at room temperature. Store in refrigerator. Serves 6–8.

Mexican Brown Rice

1½ Tbs.	canola oil
1	white onion, chopped
3	garlic cloves, sliced
1–2	jalapeño peppers, seeded and chopped
1½ cups	long-grain brown rice
2¾ cups	water
¾ cup	canned crushed tomatoes
1 tsp.	chili powder
1 tsp.	salt

Heat oven to 350°F. In an ovenproof saucepan, heat oil over medium-high heat. Add onion, garlic, and jalapeño peppers and cook, stirring often, about 4 minutes. Stir in rice and cook 1 minute. Add water, tomatoes, chili powder, and salt. Bring to a boil, stir, and cover. Place in oven and bake, without stirring, until rice is tender, about 1 hour. Fluff with a fork and serve.

Chipotle Potatoes

2 cups	heavy cream
1 Tbs.	chipotle pepper in adobo sauce, puréed
3 med.	baking potatoes, peeled and thinly sliced ⅛-inch thick
	salt and freshly ground black pepper to taste

Chipotle purée also works well blended into mashed sweet potatoes. Add 1½ tablespoons of the purée per 6 servings of mashed potatoes.

Preheat oven to 375°F. Lightly grease a 9 x 9 casserole dish. Whisk together cream and chipotle purée until smooth. Place 1 layer of potatoes in bottom of dish. Drizzle with 3 tablespoons of cream mixture and season with salt and pepper. Repeat with the remaining potatoes, cream, salt, and pepper to form as many layers as possible. Cover with aluminum foil and bake for 30 minutes. Remove cover and continue baking for an additional 45–60 minutes, until cream has been absorbed and potatoes are cooked through. Top should be lightly browned.

MOPS Mom: Loaded Mashed Potatoes

■ *Lauren Sarnoff Atwaters, Jacksonville, Florida* ■

As a child, Lauren wanted to be an artist or chef when she grew up. "I was blessed not only with an amazing family, but also to be able to live out both of my childhood dreams," Lauren said. "I am a work-at-home mom who makes art for a living and gets to cook just about every day."

Lauren came up with the idea for this recipe while eating a loaded baked potato at a restaurant many years ago. "One night I was cooking regular mashed potatoes and decided to make it a little more fun by loading them up," Lauren said.

Because her daughter sometimes has low iron levels, Lauren often mixes in a prepared package of creamed spinach (such as Stouffer's) she has warmed. Her kids love eating spinach this way!

3½ cups	chicken broth
5 lg.	potatoes, peeled and cut into 1-inch cubes
½ cup	heavy cream
½ cup	sour cream
2 Tbs.	unsalted butter
¼ cup	fresh chives, chopped
4	bacon slices, cooked and crumbled
	pepper to taste
	shredded cheese, if desired

Bring broth to a boil. Add potatoes and reduce heat to medium. When potatoes are tender, drain, but save the broth. Mash potatoes, adding back in ¼ cup broth and remaining ingredients. Garnish with extra bacon and cheese, if desired.

Goat Cheese Mashed Potatoes

3 lbs.	russet potatoes, peeled and cut into chunks
1 cup	milk
1 sm.	yellow onion, chopped
6 Tbs.	unsalted butter
4 oz.	soft fresh goat cheese, crumbled
	salt and black pepper to taste

Cook potatoes in large pot of boiling salted water until tender, about 30 minutes. Meanwhile, bring milk, onion, and butter to boil in small saucepan over medium-high heat. Remove from heat. Drain potatoes and return to pot. Add hot milk mixture and mash. Add goat cheese and mash until blended. Season to taste with salt and pepper. Serves 6.

Mashed Potatoes with Fresh Corn

2 lg.	potatoes, peeled and cubed
5 Tbs.	unsalted butter
½ cup	milk
4	garlic cloves, minced
1 cup	fresh corn kernels
2 tsp.	chili powder
1 tsp.	fresh cilantro, chopped
1 tsp.	honey
	salt to taste

In saucepan, place potatoes with enough water to cover by 2 inches. Bring to boil; reduce heat and simmer 15–20 minutes, until tender. Drain thoroughly. Meanwhile, in small skillet, melt butter in milk. Bring to boil; add garlic and corn. Reduce heat and let simmer 3 minutes. Sprinkle in chili powder. Strain mixture, reserving liquid. Place cooked potatoes in large mixing bowl. With electric mixer, whip potatoes while drizzling in reserved liquid. When consistency is right, stir in corn, cilantro, and honey. Season with salt.

Rosemary New Potatoes

3 lbs.	new potatoes, washed and halved
2 Tbs.	olive oil
1 tsp.	salt
	black pepper to taste
1 Tbs.	fresh rosemary, chopped

Preheat oven to 450°F. In a large bowl, stir together potatoes, olive oil, salt, and black pepper to taste. Line a baking sheet with foil. Spread potatoes in an even layer on the sheet. Sprinkle with rosemary. Roast for 35 minutes, stirring once, until potatoes are cooked through and browned. Serves 6–8.

Gruyère Potato Gratin

2 lbs.	Yukon gold potatoes
2 med.	onions, thinly sliced
1	garlic clove, minced
2 Tbs.	unsalted butter
1 cup	heavy cream or half-and-half
	salt and pepper to taste
¾ lb.	Gruyère cheese, shredded

Preheat oven to 350°F. Boil whole potatoes for 10 minutes; remove from heat and allow to cool to room temperature. In the meantime, sauté onions and garlic in butter until soft and translucent. Slice potatoes and layer with onions in a 9 x 9 baking dish. Pour cream over potatoes. Season to taste with salt and pepper and sprinkle Gruyère over the whole shebang. Bake 40–50 minutes or until golden.

Snap Peas and New Potatoes

8 sm.	new red potatoes
1 lb.	sugar snap peas
6 Tbs.	apple cider vinegar
2 Tbs.	fresh dill, minced
½ tsp.	salt
½ tsp.	black pepper
½ cup	olive oil
6	green onions, chopped

Place potatoes in a large pot. Cover with water and boil 25 minutes, until tender. In the last 2 minutes of cooking, add peas. Drain. When cool enough to handle, slice potatoes thinly. Add to peas in serving bowl. Combine vinegar, dill, salt, and pepper in a small bowl. Whisk in oil. Pour over peas and potatoes. Mix together, adding green onions. Serve immediately, or refrigerate and serve cold. Serves 6.

Broccoli and Cashew Stir-Fry

1 Tbs.	olive oil
1	garlic clove, crushed
½ cup	unsalted cashew nuts
3 cups	raw broccoli, cut into small florets
	salt to taste

If you prefer your broccoli less crisp, you can steam the florets for 3–4 minutes before adding to the skillet.

Heat oil in a heavy nonstick pan over medium-high heat. Add garlic and cashew nuts. Cook and stir over medium heat 2 minutes, or until lightly golden. Add broccoli and stir-fry 3–4 minutes, or until just tender. Sprinkle with salt to taste. Serve hot.

Broccoli and Green Bean Duo

8 cups	broccoli florets
½ lb.	fresh green beans, trimmed
½ cup	olive oil
3	garlic cloves, thinly sliced
1 tsp.	crushed red pepper flakes, or to taste
½ tsp.	salt
½ tsp.	black pepper

Steam broccoli and green beans until crisp-tender. Heat oil in a large skillet over medium-high heat. Add garlic and ½ teaspoon red pepper flakes. Sauté 30 seconds. Remove garlic and discard. Add vegetables to oil. Sauté until heated through, about 5 minutes. Season with additional red pepper flakes if desired, salt, and black pepper. Serve warm. Makes 4 servings.

Roasted Balsamic Asparagus

1 lb.	fresh asparagus, cleaned and trimmed
4 tsp.	olive oil
1 Tbs.	balsamic vinegar
½ tsp.	salt
⅛ tsp.	ground black pepper

Preheat oven to 425°F. Line a large baking sheet with foil and arrange asparagus in a single layer on the sheet. Drizzle olive oil over asparagus and roll gently to coat. Roast for 15–20 minutes, until tender. Toss roasted asparagus with balsamic vinegar, salt, and pepper; serve immediately. Serves 6.

Parmesan Tomatoes

¼ cup	unsalted butter
½ cup	fine dry bread crumbs
½ cup	Parmesan cheese, grated
1 tsp.	salt, or to taste
⅛ tsp.	pepper
3 lg.	tomatoes, peeled and cut into 1-inch slices

Preheat oven broiler and line a baking sheet with foil. Spray foil with nonstick cooking spray. Melt butter. Put half in a small bowl and stir in bread crumbs, Parmesan cheese, salt, and pepper. Brush tomato slices with remaining butter. Dip both sides in crumb mixture. Arrange on baking sheet. Broil 5–6 inches from heat until lightly browned, about 3 minutes. Turn with a spatula and brown other side. Serve hot. Serves 6.

Summer Tomato Cheese Tart

1 (9 in.)	prepared pie crust
3	ripe tomatoes, peeled and sliced
	salt and pepper to taste
2 tsp.	fresh basil, chopped
2 Tbs.	green onion, chopped
1 cup	mayonnaise
1 cup	cheddar cheese, shredded

Preheat oven to 350°F. To prebake pie crust, line with parchment paper or foil and fill ⅔ full with pie weights, dry beans, or uncooked rice. Bake for 20 minutes, then remove from oven and carefully remove weights and paper or foil. Poke a few holes in bottom of crust with a fork and return to oven for ten minutes. Let cool before filling.

Fill bottom of crust with thick slices of tomatoes. Combine remaining ingredients. Spread over tomatoes. Bake at 350°F for 30 minutes. Serve immediately. Serves 6.

Refried Black Beans

1 (15 oz.) can	black beans, undrained
1 Tbs.	fresh lime juice
1 Tbs.	sour cream or plain Greek yogurt
1 tsp.	cumin
½ tsp.	salt

In a food processor, combine all ingredients and purée until smooth. Heat in a saucepan over low heat, stirring occasionally, until heated through, about 5–10 minutes.

Garlic Citrus Spinach

2 Tbs.	canola oil
1 lg.	garlic clove, thinly sliced
3 Tbs.	orange juice
1 (10 oz.) bag	fresh baby spinach leaves
	salt and pepper to taste

In a large skillet, heat oil over medium-high heat. Add garlic and stir constantly for 30 seconds. Add orange juice and cook for another 30 seconds. Add spinach. Stir constantly until spinach wilts. Remove from heat and season with salt and pepper. Serve immediately.

Sesame Spinach

3 Tbs.	sesame oil, divided
1 Tbs.	garlic, minced
1 lb.	baby spinach
1 Tbs.	sugar
1 Tbs.	soy sauce
	salt to taste
1 Tbs.	toasted sesame seeds

Heat 2 tablespoons sesame oil in a large skillet over medium heat. Add garlic and cook 30 seconds. Add spinach and cook, stirring occasionally, until spinach is completely wilted. Reduce heat to low. Stir in sugar and soy sauce. Remove from heat. Add salt to taste. Serve hot, drizzled with remaining sesame oil and sprinkled with sesame seeds.

Homemade Cranberry Sauce

1 (12 oz.) bag	fresh cranberries
¾ cup	orange juice
⅔ cup	brown sugar
⅓ cup	sugar

Place all ingredients in a saucepan and cook over medium-high heat for 15–20 minutes, stirring occasionally. Liquid will reduce and cranberries will start to pop open. Remove from heat and serve warm. Cranberry sauce can be made ahead and stored in refrigerator, and brought to room temperature or slightly heated before serving.

Dilled Lemon Carrots

¼ cup	yellow onion, finely chopped
1½ lbs.	carrots, peeled and sliced
4 Tbs.	unsalted butter, divided
½ cup	water
½ tsp.	salt
1 tsp.	sugar
1 Tbs.	fresh lemon juice
1 tsp.	dill
pinch	white pepper

In a medium sauté pan, cook onion and carrots in 2 tablespoons butter until vegetables are softened. Add water and salt. Simmer 10 minutes. Pour off liquid. Set vegetables aside. In a small saucepan, melt remaining butter. Add sugar, lemon juice, dill, and white pepper. Toss carrots in butter mixture. Heat thoroughly. Serves 6–8.

Molasses Barbecue Beans

1 lb.	bacon, diced
2	red bell peppers, seeded and diced
2	yellow onions, diced
16 oz.	nonalcoholic beer
1 cup	purchased barbecue sauce
1 cup	brown sugar
1 cup	molasses
2 (15 oz.) cans	pinto beans, drained and rinsed

Preheat oven to 375°F. Spray a 9 x 13 casserole dish with nonstick cooking spray. Place bacon, peppers, and onions in a nonstick skillet over medium heat and cook, stirring occasionally, until bacon is cooked through and vegetables are softened. Drain excess grease. In a separate bowl, combine beer, barbecue sauce, brown sugar, and molasses. Mix well. Add beans and bacon mixture to sauce and stir to mix well. Pour into casserole dish. Bake for 45 minutes or until bubbling.

Pesto Quinoa

1 cup	quinoa, rinsed and drained
2 cups	chicken broth
2 Tbs.	basil pesto
1	tomato, diced
	salt and pepper to taste

Quinoa is pronounced "keen-wah."

Bring quinoa and chicken broth to a boil in a saucepan; cover, reduce heat to low, and simmer until moisture is completely absorbed, about 15 minutes. Remove from heat and stir in pesto. Fold in tomato. Season with salt and pepper to taste.

Quinoa Pilaf with Sun-Dried Tomatoes

1 Tbs.	unsalted butter
1 Tbs.	olive oil
1	shallot, minced
2	garlic cloves, minced
¼ cup	sun-dried tomatoes, chopped
½ cup	quinoa, rinsed well and drained
1 cup	chicken stock
¼ cup	fresh cilantro, chopped

Heat butter and olive oil in a saucepan over medium heat. Add shallots and sauté until softened. Add garlic and sauté 1 minute. Add tomatoes and quinoa and stir well. Continue to sauté until quinoa is toasted and has a wonderful aroma, about 15 minutes. Add chicken stock and bring to a boil. Reduce heat, cover, and simmer until liquid is absorbed, about 13–15 minutes. Stir in cilantro and serve.

Apple Cider Turnips

3 Tbs.	unsalted butter, divided
2 lbs.	turnips, peeled and cut into sticks
⅔ cup	apple cider
3 Tbs.	brown sugar
	sea salt and pepper to taste
2 Tbs.	fresh parsley, chopped

Preheat oven to 400°F. Grease a 9 x 13 baking dish with 1 tablespoon butter, then arrange turnips in dish in a single layer. Combine remaining 2 tablespoons butter, cider, sugar, sea salt, and pepper in a small saucepan and cook over medium heat until well combined. Pour this mixture evenly over turnips. Cover dish with foil and bake for 20 minutes. Stir turnips and continue to bake, uncovered, stirring occasionally, until fork-tender and liquid has reduced, 20–30 minutes more. Sprinkle with parsley and serve.

Herbed Lentils

1 Tbs.	olive oil
1 med.	yellow onion, chopped
1	carrot, chopped
3 cups	water
1 cup	green lentils, rinsed
1	bay leaf
1 tsp.	dried thyme
	salt and pepper to taste

In a medium saucepan, heat olive oil over medium heat. Add onion and cook until softened, stirring frequently, about 5 minutes. Add remaining ingredients and bring to a boil. Simmer until lentils are tender, about 25 minutes. Remove bay leaf, season to taste, and serve.

Glazed Brussels Sprouts with Bacon

4	bacon slices
1 (14 oz.) can	chicken broth
1 Tbs.	brown sugar
1 tsp.	salt
1½ lbs.	Brussels sprouts, trimmed and halved

Cook bacon in a Dutch oven or saucepan over medium heat for 10 minutes or until crisp. Remove bacon and drain on paper towels, reserving drippings in Dutch oven. Add broth, brown sugar, and salt to drippings and bring to a boil. Stir in Brussels sprouts. Cover and cook 6–8 minutes, or until tender. Transfer Brussels sprouts to a serving bowl using a slotted spoon, and sprinkle with crumbled bacon. Serve immediately.

Balsamic Roasted Beets

2 lbs.	med. red beets, scrubbed, green tops removed
	olive oil
	salt
½ cup	balsamic vinegar
2 tsp.	sugar
	freshly ground black pepper

Preheat oven to 400°F. Line a roasting pan with aluminum foil. Place beets in pan. Rub olive oil over beets and sprinkle with salt. Cover beets with another sheet of foil. Roast for 1–2 hours until tender, depending on size of beets. Test beets by poking with a fork. Remove from oven. While beets are cooling, heat balsamic vinegar and sugar in a saucepan over high heat, stirring frequently, until syrupy. Remove from heat. Gently peel beets and cut into chunks. Pour balsamic glaze over beets and sprinkle with pepper. Serve immediately.

My Favorite Hot Rolls

1 (.25 oz.) pkg.	rapid rise yeast
2 cups	warm water
½ cup	sugar
1 tsp.	salt
3 Tbs.	unsalted butter, melted
4–5 cups	all-purpose flour

Dissolve yeast in warm water. Stir in sugar and salt. Add 4 cups of flour and mix well. You may need to add up to another cup of flour to make a firm dough that is not sticky. Place in a greased bowl; cover and let rise in a warm place until double in size, about 1½–2 hours. Turn dough out onto a floured work surface and roll ½-inch thick. Cut dough with a biscuit cutter, without twisting. Dip each roll in melted butter. Fold each roll in half and place in a 9 x 13 baking pan that has been sprayed with nonstick cooking spray or 2 round cake pans. Cover and let rise again until doubled in size, about 30–45 minutes. Preheat oven to 425°F. Bake rolls for 15–20 minutes until golden brown. Makes 20 rolls.

Rolls may be flash-frozen on a cookie sheet after shaped and dipped in butter, and stored in a freezer bag. To use, place frozen rolls on prepared pan. Cover with a cloth and let rise in a warm place 2 hours. Bake as directed.

Cheddar Cayenne Biscuits

3 cups	buttermilk baking mix (such as Pioneer)
½ tsp.	cayenne pepper
½ cup	sharp cheddar cheese, shredded
1 cup	milk

In a bowl, combine baking mix, cayenne pepper, and cheese. Stir in milk just until moistened. Turn out on a lightly floured surface and knead 3 times. Roll ¾-inch thick. Cut with a floured 2-inch biscuit cutter. Place 1 inch apart on ungreased baking sheet. Bake at 400°F for 13–15 minutes or until golden brown. Makes 9–12 biscuits.

Southern Corn Bread Dressing

3 cups	celery, chopped
2 cups	yellow onion, chopped
1 cup	unsalted butter
4 cups	crumbled corn bread (can make from a mix)
3 cups	torn white bread
2 Tbs.	poultry seasoning
1 Tbs.	dried sage, optional
1 tsp.	salt
1 Tbs.	black pepper
2	eggs, beaten
8 cups	chicken broth

Preheat oven to 350°F. In a large skillet, sauté celery and onion in butter until softened, but not brown. Combine crumbled corn bread and white bread in a large mixing bowl. Add celery mixture, poultry seasoning, sage, salt, and pepper. Mix well. Add more salt and pepper if needed. Add eggs and mix well. Stir in enough broth to make a fairly thin mixture. It will be thinner than you think it should be, but the corn bread soaks up the broth. Spoon dressing into a large baking pan sprayed with nonstick cooking spray. Bake for 1 hour. Serve immediately. Serves 8–10.

Smoked Gouda Macaroni and Cheese

1 lb.	macaroni shells, cooked according to pkg. directions
¼ cup	unsalted butter
¼ cup	all-purpose flour
4 cups	milk
½ tsp.	salt
½ tsp.	black pepper
2 cups	sharp white cheddar cheese, grated
2 cups	smoked Gouda cheese, grated
½ tsp.	paprika

Preheat oven to 400°F. Melt butter in a large saucepan over medium-low heat; whisk in flour until smooth. Continue whisking and cook for 2 minutes. Gradually whisk in milk. Whisking constantly, cook for 5 minutes or until thickened and bubbly. Reduce heat to low and stir in salt, black pepper, and most of the cheese, reserving about ½ cup of each cheese. Pour pasta into a lightly greased 8 x 11 x 2 baking dish. Spoon cheese sauce over pasta, stirring lightly to even out the sauce in the pan. Sprinkle the top with remaining cheese and paprika. Bake for 20 minutes or until bubbly. Serves 8.

Garlic Cheese Grits

5 cups	water
1 tsp.	salt
1¼ cups	uncooked quick-cooking grits
1 cup	sharp cheddar cheese, shredded
1 cup	Monterey Jack cheese, shredded
½ cup	half-and-half
1 Tbs.	unsalted butter
½ tsp.	garlic powder
¼ tsp.	pepper

Bring water and salt to a boil in a medium saucepan over medium-high heat. Gradually whisk in grits; bring to a boil. Reduce heat to medium-low and simmer, stirring occasionally, 10 minutes or until thickened. Stir in cheeses and remaining ingredients until cheese is melted and mixture is well blended. Serve immediately. Serves 6.

Roasted Garlic Dipping Oil for Italian Bread

4	heads garlic, roasted (see recipe below)
½ cup	olive oil
¼ cup	balsamic vinegar
	salt and pepper to taste
1 med. loaf	crusty Italian bread

Smear 3 tablespoons of roasted garlic in the bottom of a shallow dish. Drizzle with olive oil and balsamic vinegar. Sprinkle with salt and pepper to taste. Serve with hot Italian bread.

For the roasted garlic:

4	heads of garlic
½ cup	olive oil
2 tsp.	coarse sea salt
1 tsp.	ground black pepper

Preheat oven to 400°F. Place baking sheet in oven while it preheats. Peel off the outermost layers of each head of garlic, but leave a few layers so the head stays together. Using a sharp knife, cut the top off the heads, which will expose a little bit of each garlic clove. Place the whole heads on a piece of foil, and drizzle each with olive oil, salt, and pepper. Seal foil well. Place on heated baking sheet and roast 40 minutes or until very tender. When cool enough to handle, squeeze garlic pulp from heads.

CHAPTER 9

Proportion Distortion

Childhood and adult obesity rates are on the rise, and I know you want to do everything you can to give your family the healthiest, yet still most delicious, choices possible. Sure, there are nights when you have to order your dinner through your car window, but fast food should be the exception, not the rule, for how you feed your kids.

One easy thing you can do to help your family make healthier choices is to simply pay attention to the size of the portions you give them on their dinner plates. For example, it might come as a surprise that the amount of potato for one serving is about the same size as a tennis ball. And no, I'm not talking about one bite—I'm talking about your whole meal.

Or take a golf ball. All the peanut butter you need for one serving is the size of that little white ball.

Learning to eat slower and with smaller portions is not easy at first because we think we have to eat until our eyes cross before we will feel satisfied. But did you know it takes our brains twenty minutes to send the rest of the body a message that we are full? Drink a glass of water before you eat and drink water while you eat, and you'll be surprised to find you are actually full before you know it.

Here are a few handy tips to remember when preparing your family plates. Learning to "eyeball" the amount of food you really need will go a long way toward helping your family maintain a healthy lifestyle.

Food Family Style

One Serving of . . .	Equals . . .
meat, poultry, fish	deck of cards (about three ounces)
pancakes	one pancake about the size of a CD
peanut butter	golf ball
fruit	baseball
cereal	what you can hold in your hand (¾ cup)
cheese	six dice
potato	computer mouse or tennis ball

A portion and a serving are not the same! A portion is how much you want to eat, which may be three times as much as the recommended serving. Stick with appropriate serving sizes and you very likely will stay at your optimal weight.

One more thing: don't eat while you watch TV! A distracted brain does not pay attention to what its mouth is doing. People eat four to five times more than they think they do while watching an entertaining show and eating a bag of potato chips. If you enjoy eating while you watch TV, don't take the whole bag to the den.

CHAPTER 10

Desserts

Dad is great! He gives us chocolate cake!

Bill Cosby, comedian

You can tell a lot about someone if you know his or her favorite foods and favorite music. I've also never understood it when people tell me that food and music don't mean anything to them.

For me, this world makes a bit of sense because of its beautiful food, poetry, art, and music, which I believe God created for us to not only enjoy, but also as a way for us to find him in our midst. I tell people all the time that God is definitely a chef.

I have tried to share my passion for good food and music with my sons, wanting to share with them their first experience of a perfect steak or their first live concert.

I think music must be what feelings sound like. One song can take you back to your first kiss, and another can get you dancing in the kitchen while you and your kids cook dinner. Certain songs make me cry every single time I hear them, and others remind me that I am never alone in this crazy, mixed-up world.

The power good food and music have to move us is often overlooked because of their familiarity in our busy lives. We eat, but don't taste. We hear, but have forgotten how to listen.

Life is short, and yes, it can be overwhelmingly difficult at times. Sometimes the only sound I hear is a deafening silence. But still, there is much to enjoy along the way—you just have to grab it whenever and however you can. Bite into dark chocolate, and let it melt on your tongue. Close your eyes and listen to the sounds of Sara Groves. Yes, you can survive without knowing these simple pleasures, but why? Wouldn't it be much more fun to eat, sing, and dance all the way home?

God in our waking, God in our speaking;
God in our cooking, God in our eating;
God in our playing, God in our digesting;
God in our working, God in our resting.

Apple Crumb Pie with Cinnamon Cream Sauce

For the pie:

1 (9 in.)	unbaked pie crust, chilled
1 cup	all-purpose flour, sifted
½ cup	brown sugar, firmly packed
⅛ tsp.	salt
½ cup	unsalted butter, softened
6 cups	tart apples, peeled and sliced
½ cup	granulated sugar
1 tsp.	cinnamon

For the sauce:

1½ cups	sugar
⅔ cup	light corn syrup
⅓ cup	water
1½ tsp.	cinnamon
⅔ cup	evaporated milk

Preheat oven to 375°F. Combine flour, brown sugar, salt, and butter. Blend with a fork until crumbly. Set aside. Combine apples, granulated sugar, and cinnamon; mix gently with apple slices to coat. Pack apple mixture into chilled pie crust. Sprinkle crumb topping over apples. Bake until apples are tender, about 50 minutes. While baking, prepare sauce. Bring sugar, light corn syrup, water, and cinnamon to a boil over medium heat. Boil 4 minutes. Cool for 10 minutes. Stir in evaporated milk. Serve pie warm with vanilla ice cream and cinnamon cream sauce. Serves 8.

MOPS Mom: Frozen Lemonade Pie

■ *Kelly Harrah, Fayetteville, Georgia* ■

Kelly received a similar recipe for lemonade pie from a friend but decided she would change it a little and freeze it since her family loves ice cream. It turned out perfectly!

"I love to cook," Kelly said. "I did a few things very young to help my mother. When I was about twelve, my job was to make the spaghetti sauce when my mom and dad were at work, and when I moved out on my own at eighteen, I just loved to experiment with cooking."

12 oz.	whipped topping, thawed
8 oz.	frozen lemonade concentrate (regular or pink), thawed
1 (14 oz.) can	sweetened condensed milk
1	purchased graham cracker crust

To make an orange "dreamsicle" pie, use frozen orange juice concentrate instead of lemonade. Frozen limeade concentrate is delicious too!

Stir together whipped topping, lemonade concentrate, and condensed milk. Pour in crust and freeze until firm, at least 4 hours.

Southern Pecan Pie

1 (9 in.)	pie crust, unbaked
¼ cup	unsalted butter, softened
1 cup	sugar
4 lg.	eggs
¾ cup	light corn syrup
2 tsp.	vanilla extract
1½ cups	pecan halves

Try sprinkling ½ cup chocolate chips on the bottom of the pie crust before pouring filling over!

Preheat oven to 400°F. Cream butter and sugar together using an electric mixer. Beat in eggs. Stir in corn syrup and vanilla. Add pecans and mix thoroughly. Pour filling into prepared pie crust. Bake 5 minutes at 400°F, then reduce heat to 325°F and continue baking until done, about 45 minutes.

Lime or Lemon Ice Box Pie

1¼ cups	graham cracker crumbs (9 whole crackers)
2 Tbs.	sugar
pinch	salt
5 Tbs.	unsalted butter, melted
1 (14 oz.) can	sweetened condensed milk
4 lg.	egg yolks
½ cup + 2 Tbs.	fresh lime or lemon juice
¾ cup	whipping cream
1 Tbs.	powdered sugar

Preheat oven to 350°F. Stir together graham cracker crumbs, sugar, salt, and butter until combined well, then press mixture evenly into bottom and up sides of a 9-inch glass pie plate. Bake crust in middle of oven for 10 minutes and cool on a rack. Whisk together condensed milk and egg yolks until combined well. Add lemon or lime juice and whisk until combined. Pour filling into crust and bake in middle of oven for 15 minutes. Cool pie completely on rack, then chill, covered, at least 8 hours. Just before serving, beat cream and powdered sugar in a bowl with an electric mixer until it just holds stiff peaks. Serve pie topped with whipped cream.

Chocolate Chess Pie

1 (9 in.)	pie crust, unbaked
1½ cups	sugar
3 Tbs.	baking cocoa
2	eggs
¼ cup	unsalted butter, melted
1 (5 oz.) can	evaporated milk
1 tsp.	vanilla extract

Preheat oven to 350°F. Sift sugar and cocoa together. Add eggs and butter. Mix well. Mix in evaporated milk and vanilla. Pour into prepared pie shell and bake for 30 minutes.

Chocolate Chip Pie

1 (9 in.)	pie crust, unbaked
2	eggs
½ cup	all-purpose flour
1 cup	sugar
½ cup	unsalted butter, melted and cooled
1 cup	pecans, optional
1 cup	chocolate chips
1 tsp.	vanilla extract

Preheat oven to 350°F. Beat eggs, then add flour and sugar to mix well. Add melted butter and mix again. Fold in nuts, if using, chocolate chips, and vanilla. Pour into unbaked pie crust. Bake for 30 minutes. Serve warm with whipped cream.

Old-Fashioned Buttermilk Pie

1 (9 in.)	pie crust, unbaked
½ cup	buttermilk
1⅔ cups	sugar
¼ cup	unsalted butter, melted
3	eggs, beaten lightly
1 tsp.	vanilla extract
¼ tsp.	cinnamon

Preheat oven to 350°F. Blend buttermilk, sugar, and butter. Add eggs and mix well. Blend in vanilla and cinnamon. Pour into unbaked pie crust. Bake 45 minutes, until golden brown.

Pumpkin Pie with Walnut Streusel Topping

1 (9 in.)	pie crust, unbaked
1 cup	light brown sugar, packed
2 lg.	eggs, room temperature
½ tsp.	salt
½ tsp.	cinnamon
½ tsp.	ground ginger
¼ tsp.	ground cloves
1 cup	canned pumpkin purée
1 cup	heavy whipping cream

For the topping:

½ cup	walnut pieces
½ cup	brown sugar, packed
½ tsp.	cinnamon
⅛ tsp.	salt

Preheat oven to 350°F. Press pie crust into a 9-inch pie plate. Crimp edges as desired. Bake crust for 15 minutes, using a liner of waxed paper and pie weights, dry beans, or rice in bottom of pie crust to help set crust. Remove waxed paper and weights, and poke a few holes with a fork in the bottom of crust. Continue to bake 10 more minutes. Cool on wire rack.

For filling, whisk together brown sugar, eggs, salt, cinnamon, ginger, and cloves. Add pumpkin and cream. Whisk until well blended. Pour into crust and bake 30 minutes, until filling is set. Cover edges of crust with foil if necessary to prevent overbrowning.

Meanwhile, to make topping, combine walnuts, brown sugar, cinnamon, and salt in food processor or blender. Blend to crumbs. After pie has baked 30 minutes, reduce oven temperature to 325°F. Sprinkle with topping and continue to bake 15 more minutes until completely set. Transfer to wire rack to cool completely. If not serving the same day, refrigerate. Return to room temperature before serving.

Easy Fruit Cobbler

1¼ cups	sugar, divided
1 cup	self-rising flour
1 cup	milk
½ cup	unsalted butter, melted
2 cups	fruit (blackberries, blueberries, sliced peaches), rinsed and patted dry

Preheat oven to 350°F. Spray a shallow square casserole dish or pie plate with nonstick cooking spray. Pour 1 cup sugar and flour into a mixing bowl. Add milk and whisk well. Pour in melted butter and whisk well. Pour batter into prepared baking dish. Sprinkle fruit over batter, distributing evenly. Sprinkle remaining ¼ cup sugar over the top. Bake for 1 hour, until golden and bubbly. Serve warm with vanilla ice cream, if desired.

Gluten Free Berry Crisp

6 cups	mixed berries (thawed if frozen)
¾ cup	light brown sugar, divided
¼ cup	minute tapioca
juice of ½	lemon
1 tsp.	ground cinnamon
6 Tbs.	unsalted butter, cut into pieces
½ cup	rice flour
½ cup	sliced almonds

Preheat oven to 375°F. Spray an 8- or 9-inch square baking pan with nonstick cooking spray. Place berries in a large bowl. Add ½ cup brown sugar, tapioca, lemon juice, and cinnamon. Stir well. Let stand while you prepare the topping. Place butter, remaining ¼ cup brown sugar, and rice flour in a food processor. Pulse until coarse crumbs form. Add almonds. Pulse again until combined, leaving some larger pieces of almonds. Transfer berry mixture to prepared pan. Sprinkle topping over berries. Bake 20–30 minutes or until topping is browned and filling is bubbly. Serves 8–9.

Rustic Apple Tart

1 (9 in.)	pie crust, unbaked
3–4	apples, roughly chopped
6 Tbs.	sugar
1 Tbs.	cornstarch
1 tsp.	cinnamon
½ tsp.	nutmeg
¼ cup + 2 Tbs.	unsalted butter
	sugar for sprinkling, preferably Turbinado or large crystal variety

Heat oven to 400° F. Place pie crust in an 8- or 9-inch cast-iron skillet, allowing dough to hang over the edges. In a bowl, combine apples, sugar, cornstarch, and spices. Mix until apples are thoroughly coated. Fill pie crust with the apple mixture, piling it high in the middle. Gently fold the dough edges in toward the center. Cut ¼ cup of butter into cubes. Dot apples with butter pats. Melt remaining 2 tablespoons butter and brush onto the crust. Sprinkle additional sugar over apples and crust as desired. Bake for 30–40 minutes, or until crust is brown and sugar has melted. Serve warm.

MOPS Favorite: Chocolate Peanut Butter Bars

1 pkg. (⅓ box)	graham crackers, crushed fine
1 cup	unsalted butter, melted
1 cup	peanut butter, smooth or crunchy
2⅔ cups	powdered sugar
1 cup	chocolate chips

Mix crushed graham crackers, butter, peanut butter, and powdered sugar together. Spread evenly into a 9 x 13 pan. Melt chocolate chips and spread over top. Using a knife, score chocolate layer into 36 equal bars and refrigerate 2–3 hours. Run a sharp knife under hot water; dry. Following score marks, cuts bars into squares. Serves 36.

All-American Chocolate Chip Cookies

2 cups	all-purpose flour
½ tsp.	baking soda
½ tsp.	salt
¾ cup	unsalted butter, softened
1 cup	brown sugar, packed
½ cup	white sugar
1 tsp.	vanilla extract
1	egg
1	egg yolk
2 cups	semisweet chocolate chips

Preheat oven to 325°F. Grease cookie sheets or line with parchment paper.

Sift together flour, baking soda, and salt; set aside. In a medium bowl, cream together butter, brown sugar, and white sugar until well blended. Beat in the vanilla, egg, and egg yolk until light and creamy. Mix in the sifted ingredients until just blended.

Stir in chocolate chips by hand using a wooden spoon. Drop cookie dough ¼ cup at a time (for giant cookies) or a tablespoon at a time (for smaller cookies) onto prepared cookie sheets. Cookies should be about 3 inches apart. Bake 15–17 minutes for larger cookies and 10–12 minutes for smaller ones, until edges are lightly browned. Cool on baking sheets for a few minutes before transferring to wire racks to cool completely.

Homemade Brownies

4 (1 oz.) sq.	unsweetened baking chocolate
¾ cup	unsalted butter
2 cups	sugar
3	eggs
1 tsp.	vanilla extract
1 cup	all-purpose flour
1 cup	chocolate chips

Preheat oven to 350°F. Microwave chocolate and butter in large bowl on high for 2 minutes or until butter is melted. Stir until chocolate is melted. Stir in sugar. Mix in eggs and vanilla. Stir in flour and chocolate chips. Spread in greased 9 x 13 pan. Bake for 35 minutes (do not overbake). Cool in pan before cutting.

MOPS Mom: Grandma Helen's Praline Wafers

■ *Leitha Harris, Frankfort, Kentucky* ■

The name of this recipe tells you where Leitha Harris first learned to make it. "The recipe came from my grandmother, Helen, and I love these," Leitha said. "Everywhere I have taken these, such as the MOPS cookie exchange, they have been a huge hit. I even won a cookie cook-off in my work building with them."

10–12	whole graham crackers
1 cup	light brown sugar
1 cup	unsalted butter
¼ cup	pecan pieces

You can add 1 cup coconut, drizzle with chocolate, or use almonds in place of pecans.

Preheat oven to 325°F. Line a rimmed 11 x 15 cookie sheet with foil, and cover in a single layer of graham crackers. In a saucepan over medium heat, combine sugar and butter, stirring to combine. Bring to a boil and cook for 3 minutes, until caramelized. Remove from heat and stir in pecan pieces. Pour mixture over graham crackers and bake for 7 minutes. Let cool, and break into squares. Store in an airtight container. Best eaten within 1–2 days.

MOPS Mom: So Simple, So Good Peanut Butter Cookies

■ *Mandie Franklin, Fort Stewart, Georgia* ■

At first glance, Mandie Franklin's cookies seem to be missing an ingredient or two. Most cookies contain flour, but these turn out perfect and delicious. Great for a quick, chewy, gluten free treat after school!

1 cup	creamy peanut butter
1 cup	sugar
1 lg.	egg

Preheat oven to 350°F. Stir well to combine ingredients and drop by teaspoonfuls at least 2 inches apart on cookie sheet. They do spread a bit, so make sure you leave room for nice-looking cookies. Use a fork to make a crisscross on the top before baking. Bake for 8 minutes. Let cool.

Easy S'More Bars

½ cup	heavy whipping cream
1 (11.5 oz.) pkg.	milk chocolate chips (or 1¾ cups)
4 cups	miniature marshmallows
½ (12.5 oz.) pkg.	graham crackers, broken into bite-size pieces

Line a 9 x 9 baking pan with foil. In a saucepan, heat cream over medium heat just until bubbles appear around edge of pan, 1–2 minutes. Remove from heat and mix in milk chocolate chips, stirring until smooth. Allow to cool, stirring occasionally, until cool to the touch. This should take only about 5 minutes. Add marshmallows to the chocolate mixture and stir gently to coat. Then gently stir in graham cracker pieces until combined. Pour the mixture into foil-lined pan, and press gently. Be sure to scrape out every last drop!

Refrigerate for 2 hours or until firm. Remove from pan using the foil and cut into bars with a knife that has been sprayed with nonstick cooking spray. Makes 9–12 bars.

Christmas Peppermint Cookies

1 cup	unsalted butter, softened
½ cup	sugar
1 lg.	egg
1 tsp.	vanilla extract
2½ cups	all-purpose flour
½ tsp.	salt
1 cup	regular oats
⅓ cup	hard peppermint candy, crushed
	powdered sugar, for dusting

If you're going to freeze these cookies, do so before icing.

For the icing:

4 cups	sifted powdered sugar
dash	salt
¼–½ cup	half-and-half
1 tsp.	peppermint extract
	red food coloring

Beat butter at medium speed until creamy; gradually add sugar, beating well. Add egg and vanilla, beating well. Combine flour and salt; add to butter mixture. Stir in oats and candy. Cover and chill 1 hour.

Preheat oven to 350°F. Line a baking sheet with foil and spray with nonstick cooking spray. Divide dough in half. Roll each portion to ⅛-inch thick on surface dusted with powdered sugar. Cut with 2-inch cookie cutter; place on prepared baking sheet. Bake for 8 minutes; remove to wire racks to cool.

For the icing: combine powdered sugar and salt. Add half-and-half until icing reaches desired consistency. Add peppermint extract. Remove ¼ cup icing and stir in 1–2 drops of food coloring for pink color.

Spread cookies with white icing. Before icing sets, drizzle lines of pink icing across the top of each cookie.

Sand Tarts

1 cup	unsalted butter, softened
½ cup	powdered sugar, sifted
2 cups	all-purpose flour, sifted
½ Tbs.	cold water
¾ tsp.	vanilla extract
1 cup	pecans, chopped
	powdered sugar, for dusting

Tip: toast your nuts before using in any recipe. It brings out great flavor!

Preheat oven to 325°F. Cream butter and powdered sugar with an electric mixer. Gradually add flour and water. Mix well. Stir in vanilla and pecans. Roll into small balls. Place on ungreased cookie sheets. Bake for 20 minutes, until lightly browned. Roll in additional powdered sugar while still warm. Makes 8 dozen. Freezes well.

Gooey Butter Cake

3	eggs
½ cup	unsalted butter, melted
1 pkg.	yellow cake mix
8 oz.	cream cheese, softened
4 cups (16 oz.)	powdered sugar

Preheat oven to 350°F. Spray a 9 x 13 baking pan with nonstick cooking spray. Combine 1 egg, melted butter, and cake mix. Pat into bottom of baking pan. Using an electric mixer, beat 2 remaining eggs with cream cheese and powdered sugar. Pour cream cheese mixture into pan. Bake 35–45 minutes. Cool in pan. Cut into squares. Store in refrigerator.

Mama's Pink Lady Cake

This is my mother's recipe, and it is one of my favorite memories from my childhood. I love this cake. I crave it and find excuses to make it whenever I can!

1 pkg.	white cake mix
3 Tbs.	sifted cake flour
1 (3 oz.) pkg.	strawberry gelatin
5 oz.	frozen sweetened strawberries, thawed
4	eggs, room temperature
1 cup	vegetable oil

For the icing:

5 oz.	frozen strawberries, thawed
4 cups (16 oz.)	powdered sugar, sifted
½ cup	unsalted butter, softened

Preheat oven to 350°F. Combine cake mix, cake flour, and gelatin in a large mixing bowl. Mix 1 tablespoon of juice from thawed berries with enough water to make ½ cup. Add to cake mix along with eggs and oil. Mix on low speed until thoroughly combined. Add strawberries and remaining juice. Blend evenly. Grease sides and bottom of 2 9-inch cake pans. Line bottoms with wax paper. Sprinkle with flour. Divide cake batter evenly between both pans. Bake at 350 degrees for 25–30 minutes, until set and golden brown. Cool on cake rack.

For icing, drain berries, reserving juice. Pour powdered sugar into mixing bowl and add softened butter, berries, and half the reserved juice. Blend on low speed of an electric mixer. Add remaining juice teaspoon by teaspoon until right spreading consistency. Frost cake and store, covered, in refrigerator until serving.

Easy Coconut Sheet Cake

1 pkg.	white cake mix
1 (15 oz.) can	cream of coconut
1 (14 oz.) can	sweetened condensed milk
8 oz.	whipped topping (or 2 cups sweetened whipped cream)
1 (12 oz.) pkg.	flaked coconut

Bake white cake according to box instructions for a 9 x 13 cake. Punch lots of holes in cake with ice pick or skewer. Gently pour cream of coconut and then condensed milk evenly over warm cake. Top with whipped topping or sweetened whipped cream and sprinkle coconut over. Store in refrigerator.

Sour Cream Pound Cake

3 cups	all-purpose flour
¼ tsp.	baking soda
1 cup	unsalted butter, softened
3 cups	sugar
6	eggs
1 cup	sour cream
1 tsp.	vanilla extract
1 tsp.	almond extract
1 tsp.	lemon extract

Preheat oven to 350°F. Grease and flour a tube pan. Sift flour with baking soda and set aside. Cream butter and sugar together in the bowl of an electric mixer. Add eggs, one at a time, scraping down sides of bowl as needed. Add flour gradually, mixing gently to incorporate. Add sour cream and extracts. Mix well. Spoon into prepared tube pan. Bake for 1½ hours. Cool on a wire rack for 5 minutes before turning out of pan to cool completely.

MOPS Mom: Ro's Strawberry Shortcake

■ *Jennifer Griffin, Marietta, Georgia* ■

Ro is Jennifer Griffin's maternal grandmother. Jennifer said that her grandmother got the recipe from her husband's co-worker many years ago. "It turned into a family classic and became Ro's Strawberry Shortcake," Jennifer said. "Then after she passed away from breast cancer, my paternal grandmother used to make it at our huge family gatherings."

Jennifer's husband is on active duty in the United States Navy. "Being military, I can't help but make my shortcake look like an American flag!" she added.

1 pkg.	white cake mix
1 lg. box	strawberry gelatin
2 cups	boiling water
2 (10 oz.) boxes	frozen strawberries, thawed
1 (3.4 oz.) box	instant vanilla pudding
8 oz.	whipped topping, thawed
	fresh strawberries and blueberries, for garnish

Make cake according to package directions for a 9 x 13 pan. While cake is baking, mix gelatin, boiling water, and strawberries together. While cake is still hot, poke holes into it with the rounded end of a wooden spoon, and pour gelatin mixture over cake. Cover and refrigerate overnight. The next day, mix instant vanilla pudding into whipped topping. Frost top of cake with pudding mixture. Top with fresh strawberries and/or blueberries.

MOPS Favorite: Slow Cooker Chocolate Lava Cake

1 pkg.	devil's food cake mix
3	eggs
⅓ cup	vegetable oil
1⅔ cups	water
1 (3.4 oz.) pkg.	instant chocolate pudding mix
2 cups	cold milk
2 cups	semisweet chocolate chips

Prepare cake batter according to package directions using eggs, oil, and water. Pour into slow cooker. Prepare chocolate pudding mix using milk as indicated in package directions. Pour over cake mix in slow cooker. Sprinkle evenly with chocolate chips. Cover and cook on high for 2½–3 hours until cake is moist but does not jiggle. Serve with ice cream or whipped cream. Serves 10–12.

New York Style Cheesecake

For the crust:

1 pkg. (⅓ box)	graham crackers
1 tsp.	cinnamon
⅓ cup	sugar
⅓ cup	unsalted butter, melted

For the filling:

3 (8 oz.) pkgs.	cream cheese, softened
1 cup	sugar
5 lg.	eggs
2 tsp.	vanilla extract

For the topping:

1 pint	sour cream
¼ cup	sugar
1 tsp.	vanilla extract
	fresh raspberries or strawberries, to garnish

Cheesecake can be frozen before adding topping and fruit.

Preheat oven to 375°F. For the crust: spray a regular-size springform pan with nonstick cooking spray. In a food processor, combine graham crackers, cinnamon, and sugar and pulse several times to make a fine crumb. Add melted butter and pulse again to combine. Spread mixture evenly along bottom and up the sides of pan, pressing down to compact.

For the filling: with an electric mixer, beat together cream cheese, sugar, and eggs. Add vanilla and combine well. Pour into crust. Bake for 45–60 minutes, until center is almost set.

For the topping: after cheesecake has completely cooled, beat together sour cream, sugar, and vanilla and spoon on top of cooled cake. Bake at 275°F for 15 minutes. Let cool and then chill at least 6 hours before serving. To serve, remove sides of springform pan, slice, and garnish with fresh fruit.

Lemon Punch Cake

1 pkg.	yellow cake mix
1 (3 oz.) pkg.	lemon gelatin
4	eggs
¾ cup	canola or vegetable oil
¾ cup	water

For the glaze:

4 cups (16 oz.)	sifted powdered sugar
¾ cup	fresh lemon juice

Preheat oven to 350°F. Spray Bundt pan with nonstick cooking spray. Mix all cake ingredients together with electric mixer on medium-high for 3 minutes. Pour into prepared pan and bake 40–50 minutes, until golden brown and toothpick inserted in center comes out clean. Let cool 10 minutes in pan. Turn out and poke holes in cake immediately with an ice pick or wooden skewer. Combine glaze ingredients. Spoon glaze over cake. Serve warm or at room temperature.

Pumpkin Spice Cake with Cream Cheese Icing

1 pkg.	spice cake mix
3	eggs
1 cup	canned pumpkin purée
½ cup	water
½ cup	vegetable oil
1 (3 oz.) pkg.	instant vanilla pudding
1 tsp.	cinnamon

*Freeze cake before icing.
Prepare icing on serving day.*

For the icing:

6 oz.	cream cheese, softened
½ cup	unsalted butter, softened
2 tsp.	vanilla extract
¼ tsp.	salt
5–6 cups	powdered sugar

Preheat oven to 350°F. Grease and flour a 10-inch Bundt pan. In a large mixing bowl, combine all cake ingredients. Beat on medium speed with electric mixer for 6 minutes. Pour into prepared pan, and bake for 45–55 minutes, until toothpick inserted in center comes out clean. Cool in pan for 10 minutes and then turn out onto wire rack to cool completely. For icing, beat together cream cheese, butter, vanilla, and salt. Gradually add powdered sugar until icing reaches desired consistency. Ice cake as desired. Store covered in refrigerator.

Apple Cake with Caramel Drizzle

4 cups	apples, peeled and chopped
2 cups	sugar
½ cup	vegetable oil
2	eggs
2 tsp.	vanilla extract
2 cups	all-purpose flour
2 tsp.	baking soda
1 tsp.	salt
2 tsp.	cinnamon
1 cup	walnuts, chopped, optional

Preheat oven to 350°F. In a large bowl, mix together apples, sugar, oil, eggs, and vanilla. In a separate bowl, combine flour, baking soda, salt, and cinnamon. Add to apple mixture and mix well. Stir in walnuts, if using. Pour into an ungreased 9 x 13 pan and bake for 60 minutes until toothpick inserted in center comes out clean.

Cake can be served plain, sprinkled with powdered sugar, or with caramel icing.

Caramel icing:

½ cup	unsalted butter
1 cup	light brown sugar
¼ cup	evaporated milk
1 tsp.	vanilla extract
¾–1 cup	powdered sugar

Mix butter, brown sugar, and evaporated milk in a saucepan and bring to a boul. Boil 1 minute, stirring constantly. Remove from heat. Whisk in vanilla and powdered sugar until you have a thick but pourable icing. Poke holes in top of cake and drizzle icing over.

Chocolate Sheet Cake

2 cups	all-purpose flour
2 cups	sugar
1 cup	unsalted butter
2 Tbs.	baking cocoa
1 cup	water
½ cup	buttermilk
2	eggs, beaten
1 tsp.	baking soda
1 tsp.	cinnamon
1 tsp.	vanilla extract

For the icing:

½ cup	unsalted butter
4 Tbs.	baking cocoa
6 Tbs.	buttermilk
1 (16 oz.) box	powdered sugar, sifted
1 tsp.	vanilla extract

Preheat oven to 400°F. In large bowl, stir together flour and sugar; set aside. Combine butter, cocoa, and water in medium saucepan and bring to a boil. Pour over flour mixture and mix well. Add buttermilk, eggs, soda, cinnamon, and vanilla and mix well. Pour into an ungreased sheet cake pan or 9 x 13 pan and bake for 20–25 minutes until toothpick inserted in center comes out clean.

For icing, melt butter in a medium saucepan. Add cocoa and buttermilk and bring to a full boil. Remove from heat; stir in powdered sugar and mix well. Add vanilla. Pour icing over cake when still very warm. Let cool.

Candy Bar Bundt Cake

4 (2.23 oz.)	Milky Way candy bars, sliced and divided
1 cup + 2 Tbs.	water, divided
1 pkg.	yellow cake mix with pudding
⅓ cup	unsalted butter, melted and cooled
3	eggs, room temperature
2 Tbs.	all-purpose flour
2 Tbs.	unsalted butter

Glaze too much? Cake can be dusted with powdered sugar instead.

Stir the slices from 2 candy bars with 2 tablespoons of water in a medium saucepan over medium heat until smooth, and remove from heat. Meanwhile generously butter and flour a 12-cup Bundt pan. Using an electric mixer, combine cake mix with melted butter, eggs, and remaining 1 cup water. Scoop out about ⅔ cup of the cake batter and combine with flour and melted candy bars. Pour remaining cake batter into prepared Bundt pan, then spoon candy bar mixture in a ring in the center of the batter, avoiding sides of pan. Swirl batter with a knife.

Bake at 350°F for 40 minutes and let cool in the pan on a rack for 25 minutes. Invert and unmold the cake. To make glaze, melt the slices from 2 remaining candy bars with butter and pour over cake. Serve warm or at room temperature.

Red Velvet Cupcakes with White Chocolate Icing

1 pkg.	German chocolate cake mix
1 (3.4 oz.) pkg.	instant vanilla pudding
1 cup	sour cream
½ cup	water
½ cup	vegetable oil
1 (1 oz.) bottle	red food coloring
3	eggs
1 cup	semisweet chocolate chips

If you're going to freeze these cupcakes, do so before adding icing.

For the icing:

12 oz.	white baking chocolate or vanilla almond bark
8 oz.	cream cheese, softened
½ cup	unsalted butter, softened
1 tsp.	vanilla extract
4 cups	powdered sugar

Preheat oven to 350°F. Line muffin tins with foil liners. Blend cake mix, pudding mix, sour cream, water, oil, food coloring, and eggs in a large bowl at low speed until moistened, about 30 seconds. Continue to beat at medium speed for 2 minutes, then fold in chocolate chips. Spoon batter into prepared tins and bake for 19–22 minutes. After cupcakes are done, cool on a wire rack for 5 minutes. Carefully remove cupcakes from tins and cool for an additional 15 minutes before frosting.

For the icing, melt white chocolate in a double boiler or microwave, stirring until smooth. Set aside to cool. Combine cream cheese with butter in a large mixing bowl and blend at low speed. Gradually add melted white chocolate, vanilla, and powdered sugar until all ingredients are combined. Beat at medium speed until frosting is fluffy.

Makes 24 regular-size cupcakes or approximately 72 miniature cupcakes.

Simply the Best Cupcakes

1½ cups	self-rising flour
1¼ cups	all-purpose flour
1 cup	unsalted butter, softened
2 cups	sugar
4 lg.	eggs, room temperature
1 cup	milk
1 tsp.	vanilla extract

If you're going to freeze these cupcakes, do so before adding icing.

For the icing:

1 cup	unsalted butter, softened
6–8 cups	powdered sugar
½ cup	milk
2 tsp.	vanilla extract

Preheat oven to 350°F. Line 2 regular 12-count muffin tins with cupcake papers. In a small bowl, combine the flours and set aside. In a large bowl, cream butter until smooth. Add sugar gradually and beat until fluffy, about 3 minutes. Add eggs 1 at a time, beating well after each addition. Add flour mixture in 3 parts, alternating with milk and vanilla. After each addition, beat until the ingredients are incorporated, but do not overbeat. Using a rubber spatula, scrape down the batter in the bowl to make sure ingredients are well blended. Carefully spoon batter into cupcake liners, filling them about ¾ full. Bake for 20–25 minutes, or until a cake tester inserted into the center of the cupcake comes out clean. Cool cupcakes in tins for 15 minutes. Remove from tins and cool completely on a wire rack before icing.

For the icing, place butter in a large mixing bowl. Add 4 cups of powdered sugar and then milk and vanilla. Beat at medium speed until smooth and creamy, about 3–5 minutes. Gradually add the remaining sugar, 1 cup at a time, beating well after each addition (about 2 minutes), until the icing reaches a good spreading consistency. You may not need to add all of the sugar. If desired, add a few drops of food coloring and mix thoroughly. Icing can be stored in an airtight container for up to 3 days. (Use and store the icing at room temperature because icing will set if chilled.) Makes 24 regular cupcakes.

Easiest Homemade Vanilla Ice Cream

1 (14 oz.) can	sweetened condensed milk
2 tsp.	vanilla extract
2 cups	heavy cream, chilled

In a medium bowl, combine condensed milk and vanilla. Set aside. Beat cream on high until stiff peaks form, about 3 minutes. Using a rubber spatula, gently fold whipped cream into condensed milk mixture. Scoop into a loaf pan, cover, and freeze until firm, at least 6 hours. Serve with an ice cream scoop. Makes 1½ quarts.

Lemon Velvet Ice Cream

1¼ cups	sugar
1 cup	milk
pinch	salt
1 cup	whipping cream
⅓ cup	lemon juice
1 tsp.	lemon peel, grated

If you double or triple this recipe, freezing times will increase.

Mix together sugar, milk, salt, and whipping cream; add lemon juice and lemon peel. Mix with electric mixer; freeze in a tightly covered container until firm, about four hours. Thaw slightly; whip with electric mixer; refreeze until firm, at least 4 hours.

Mexican Cinnamon Crisp Sundaes

3 Tbs.	unsalted butter
2 Tbs.	sugar
4 (8 in.)	flour tortillas, cut into ½-inch strips
½ tsp.	cinnamon
1 pint	vanilla ice cream
½ cup	hot fudge sauce (see recipe on p. 252)

Melt butter and sugar in a large skillet over medium heat. Add tortilla strips and cook until crisp, turning several times, about 5 minutes. Transfer to paper towel. Sprinkle with cinnamon. When ready to serve, scoop ice cream into individual bowls and top with warmed hot fudge sauce and cinnamon tortilla crisps. Serves 4.

Oreo Peppermint Ice Cream Pie

1	purchased chocolate cookie crust
1½ qts.	peppermint ice cream, softened
12	Oreo cookies, broken into bite-size pieces
½ cup	miniature chocolate chips
2 cups	whipped topping, thawed
	peppermint pieces and chocolate chips, to garnish
½ cup	hot fudge sauce (see recipe on p. 252)
½ tsp.	peppermint extract

Soften ice cream until "workable." Add Oreos and chocolate chips. Mix well. Spread evenly into crust. Top with whipped topping and sprinkle with peppermint pieces and additional chocolate chips as desired. Cover loosely with foil and return to freezer at least 2 hours before serving. To slice, use sharp knife that has been dipped in warm water. Warm hot fudge sauce and stir in peppermint extract. Drizzle each slice with warmed sauce and serve.

MOPS Favorite: Butterscotch Ice Cream Delight

½ cup	light brown sugar
1 cup	unsalted butter, melted
½ cup	plain oatmeal
1 cup	pecans, chopped
2 cups	all-purpose flour
2 (12 oz.) jars	purchased caramel sauce
½ gal.	French vanilla ice cream, softened

Preheat oven to 400°F. Mix together first five ingredients. Spread on cookie sheet. Bake 15 minutes. Crumble while hot. Spread half the crumbs into the bottom of a glass 9 x 13 pan. Set 1 caramel syrup jar in warm water to soften. Drizzle over crumbs. Spread softened ice cream over mixture. Set second jar of caramel syrup in warm water to soften. Spread over all. Top with remaining crumbs. Freeze 2 hours or until firm, and slice as needed. Serves 20.

Toffee Ice Cream Squares

1½ cups	chocolate cookie crumbs
⅓ cup	unsalted butter, melted
9 oz.	chocolate toffee candy bars, crushed
½ gal.	vanilla ice cream, softened
	hot fudge sauce, to garnish (see recipe on p. 252)

Mix together chocolate cookie crumbs and melted butter. Press into the bottom of a 9 x 13 pan. Freeze 15 minutes. Meanwhile, mix crushed candy bars with softened ice cream. Scoop into crust, spreading evenly with the back of a spoon. Return to freezer to harden, at least 2 hours. To serve, cut into squares and drizzle with warmed hot fudge sauce. Serves 8–12.

Frozen Peanut Butter Pie

1½ cups	powdered sugar
1 cup	creamy peanut butter
8 oz.	cream cheese, softened
½ tsp.	vanilla extract
8 oz.	whipped topping, thawed, or sweetened whipped cream
1 (6 oz.)	chocolate cookie or graham cracker crust
	hot fudge sauce, to garnish (see recipe on p. 252)

Blend powdered sugar, peanut butter, cream cheese, and vanilla until smooth, occasionally scraping down sides of bowl. Transfer mixture to large bowl. Fold whipped topping into peanut butter mixture half at a time. Spoon filling into crust and smooth top. Freeze until filling is firm, at least 3 hours. Can be prepared up to 1 week ahead. Cover and keep frozen. Let stand at room temperature 20 minutes and drizzle with hot fudge sauce before serving.

Mud Pie

1	chocolate cookie crust
1 gal.	coffee ice cream, softened
1½ cups	hot fudge sauce (see recipe on p. 252)
	whipped cream and slivered almonds, to garnish

Scoop softened ice cream into crust, making a tall, smooth, rounded top. Freeze until ice cream is firm, about 2 hours. Spread chilled fudge sauce over the ice cream. Freeze again, about 8 hours. To serve, slice pie into 8 pieces and serve on chilled dessert plates. Top with whipped cream and slivered almonds as desired.

Hot Fudge Sauce

¾ cup sugar
½ cup baking cocoa
⅔ cup evaporated milk
⅓ cup light corn syrup
⅓ cup unsalted butter
1 tsp. vanilla extract

For a really thick hot fudge sauce, boil for a few more minutes.

Combine sugar, cocoa, evaporated milk, and corn syrup together in medium saucepan and cook over medium heat, stirring constantly, until mixture reaches a rolling boil. Boil hard for 5 minutes to thicken. Remove from heat and stir in butter and vanilla. Makes about 2 cups. Can store in refrigerator up to 3 weeks.

MOPS Favorite: Banana Pudding

1 (5.9 oz.) box instant vanilla pudding
1 (4 oz.) pkg. cream cheese, softened
1 (14 oz.) can sweetened condensed milk
3 cups milk
12 oz. whipped topping
1 (12 oz.) box vanilla wafers
5 bananas, peeled and sliced

Combine pudding mix, cream cheese, and condensed milk. Beat with an electric mixer until smooth. Add milk and half of the whipped topping. Continue beating until mixture starts to thicken. Place a layer of vanilla wafers in the bottom of your serving dish, either a 9 x 13 casserole dish or a trifle dish. Top cookies with a layer of banana slices and pudding mixture, repeating layers all the way to the top. Your top layer should be the remaining half of the whipped topping. Refrigerate until serving time. Serves 12–16.

Buckeye Balls

2 cups	powdered sugar, sifted
¾ cup	smooth peanut butter
¼ cup	unsalted butter, melted
½ tsp.	vanilla extract
¼ tsp.	salt
1 cup	semisweet chocolate chips
½ tsp.	vegetable shortening

Combine powdered sugar, peanut butter, butter, vanilla, and salt and beat well with a wooden spoon. Roll peanut butter mixture into 1-inch balls and transfer to a wax paper–lined cookie sheet in a single layer. Freeze until firm, 15–20 minutes.

Melt chocolate chips and shortening in a small, heatproof bowl set over a small pot of simmering water, stirring often. Remove pot and bowl together from heat. Working with about 6 peanut butter balls at a time, insert a toothpick into the center of a ball and dip about three-quarters into the melted chocolate, leaving about a 1-inch circle of peanut butter visible at the top. Twirl toothpick between your finger and thumb to swirl off excess chocolate, then transfer to another wax paper–lined cookie sheet, chocolate side down. Slide out toothpick and repeat dipping process with remaining peanut butter balls, reheating chocolate as necessary.

Smooth out toothpick holes left in tops. Freeze buckeyes until firm. Buckeyes will keep, well-sealed, up to 2 weeks in the refrigerator. Serve at room temperature or chilled.

CHAPTER 11

Menus for Special Occasions

Valentine's Day Dinner

Balsamic Filet Mignon

Goat Cheese Mashed Potatoes

Broccoli Ramen Salad

My Favorite Hot Rolls

New York Style Cheesecake

Easter Breakfast

Miniature Banana Cinnamon
  Muffins

Brown Sugar Bacon

Easiest Breakfast Casserole

Honey Berry Salad

Easter Lunch

Slow Cooker Cola Ham

Loaded Mashed Potatoes

Strawberry Spinach Salad

Updated Green Bean Casserole

My Favorite Hot Rolls

Easy Coconut Sheet Cake

Mother's Day Breakfast in Bed

Orange Rolls

Eggs Gruyère

Vanilla Latte

Father's Day Dinner

Old-Fashioned Fruity Tea

Teriyaki Burgers

Homemade Baked Potato Chips

Buttermilk Cole Slaw

Toffee Ice Cream Squares

Fourth of July

Watermelon Lemonade

Easy Oven Brisket

White Barbecue Sauce

Molasses Barbecue Beans

Southwest Creamed Corn

Cheddar Cayenne Biscuits

Easy Fruit Cobbler

Food Family Style

Thanksgiving or Christmas Dinner

Easy Roasted Turkey Breast
Southern Corn Bread Dressing
Homemade Cranberry Sauce
Thanksgiving Sweet Potatoes
Green Bean Bundles
My Favorite Hot Rolls
Seven Layer Salad
Southern Pecan Pie

Christmas Brunch

Tex-Mex Breakfast Casserole
Chocolate Chip Croissants
Delicious Glazed Cranberry
    Bread
Homemade Applesauce

Birthday Dinner

Prosciutto Pinwheels
Linguine with Shrimp and Sun-
    Dried Tomatoes
Roasted Garlic Dipping Oil for
    Italian Bread
Italian Salad
Simply the Best Cupcakes

Date Night

Cheese Fondue
Beef Fondue
Chocolate-Dipped Strawberries

CHAPTER 12

Back to Basics

Kitchen and Pantry Essentials

Appliances

blender
coffeemaker
food processor
stand mixer

Knives

chef's knife
paring knife
serrated bread knife
steak knives

Cookware

8 x 8 square pan
9 x 13 casserole dish
9-inch pie plate
10-inch pie plate
Bundt pan
cookie sheets
jellyroll pan
large skillet
large soup/pasta pot
nonstick skillet
roasting pan
saucepans
small cast-iron skillet

Utensils

box grater
can opener
cutting boards
digital timer
fine-mesh strainer
garlic press
instant-read meat thermometer
kitchen scissors
ladle
locking tongs
measuring cups
measuring spoons
metal spatula

microplane grater/zester
offset metal spatula
oven thermometer
pot holders
potato masher
rubber spatula
salad spinner
salt and pepper grinders
sifter
slotted spoon
vegetable peeler
whisk
wire mesh colander
wooden spoons

Pantry

nonstick cooking spray
olive oil
sesame oil
vegetable oil
balsamic vinegar
red wine vinegar
rice vinegar
white wine vinegar
pasta (lasagna, spaghetti, macaroni, fettuccine)
brown rice
white rice
chicken broth and bouillon
   cubes

soy sauce
Worcestershire sauce
marinara sauce
tomato paste
dark corn syrup
light corn syrup
light brown sugar
granulated sugar
powdered sugar
all-purpose flour
self-rising flour
cornstarch
baking powder
baking soda
cocoa powder
chocolate chips
oats

Dry Seasonings

basil
bay leaves
black pepper
cayenne pepper
chili powder
cinnamon, ground
crushed red pepper
cumin, ground
curry powder
dill weed
garlic powder

ginger, ground	rosemary
lemon pepper seasoning	salt
onion powder	smoked paprika
oregano	tarragon
paprika	thyme

Healthy Swaps

Learning to modify a recipe to be healthier may take a bit of trial and error, but with these easy substitutions, you'll be removing the salt, sugar, and fat, but never the flavor!

Instead of . . .	Try . . .
bacon	Canadian bacon, turkey bacon
butter or oil in a baked good	applesauce to replace half the amount needed
butter or oil to prevent sticking	nonstick cooking spray
bread crumbs	rolled oats
chocolate chips or chunks	miniature chocolate chips
couscous	quinoa
cream	fat free half-and-half, evaporated skim milk
cream cheese	low fat cream cheese, Neufchatel cheese
crispy rice cereal	brown rice cereal
egg	2 egg whites, ¼ cup egg substitute
flour tortillas	corn tortillas, leaf lettuce (used as a wrap)
French fries	baked sweet potato fries
ground beef	ground turkey, ground chicken
ice cream	low fat frozen yogurt
instant oatmeal	steel-cut oats
mashed potatoes	mashed, steamed cauliflower
milk chocolate	dark chocolate
pasta	whole wheat pasta, zucchini ribbons, spaghetti squash
peanut butter	natural peanut butter, almond butter

Instead of . . .	Try . . .
potato chips	kale chips (they're delicious!), air-popped popcorn
salt	reduce by half for the amount needed, except in recipes with yeast; don't put the salt shaker on the table
sour cream	nonfat plain Greek yogurt
seasoned salt	herbs, spices, citrus juice, vinegar
sugar	Splenda (sucralose) or try reducing up to ⅓ of required sugar in baked goods and adding 1 tsp. vanilla extract, almond extract, or cinnamon
white bread	whole grain bread, whole wheat pita
white flour	whole wheat flour to replace half the amount needed
white rice	brown rice, pearl barley, quinoa, wild rice

Recipe Index

Recipe Index

265

Recipe Index

Leigh Oliver Vickery is creator and founder of Leigh Oliver's, a specialty "fun food" company with numerous products on the market in at least twenty-five states and grocery chains, including Whole Foods Market and Costco. She is the former food editor of the *Tyler Morning Telegraph* in Tyler, Texas, and is now the food and family contributor for Brookshire Grocery Company. She also blogs at www.onebighappytable.com. Leigh also has a regular twice-weekly segment on local TV stations called "One Big Happy Table with Leigh Vickery." She lives in Tyler, Texas, with her husband, two sons, and three dogs.

Meet Leigh Oliver Vickery at
www.leigholivers.com

Connect with her on

facebook Leigh Oliver Smith Vickery

twitter @leigholiver

Blog: onebighappytable.com

Like us on Facebook at "One Big Happy Table"

Want to be the best mom possible?
You are not alone.

**At MOPS you can enjoy real friendships,
personal growth, and spiritual hope
as part of a mothering community.**

Get connected today!

Mothers of Preschoolers

2370 S. Trenton Way, Denver CO 80231
888.910.MOPS

For information on MOPS International, visit **MOPS.org**

Better Moms Make a Better World

Be the First to Hear about Other New Books from Revell!

Sign up for announcements about new and upcoming titles at

www.revellbooks.com/signup

Follow us on **twitter**
RevellBooks

Join us on **facebook**
Revell

Don't miss out on our great reads!

Revell

a division of Baker Publishing Group
www.RevellBooks.com